An Explosion of Love
The Color of All Things Beautiful

by

T i g m o n k

Dedication...

This work is dedicated to my
Three Blooming Beauties...

Talia Dawn, Braya Lilly, Adella Marie

Special Thanks, to... You

Note from Tigmonk:

I feel it is wise to share with you some insight before you begin reading this book. First and foremost, from my perspective, this book is simply an exploration of my own unfolding. I did not write with the intent that it must be shared, I wrote it simply because it desired to be written. What I mean by this is it was a spontaneous occurrence: one day I started writing to understand more clearly the movement of Love in my own Heart and the final result was something beyond any expectation I had.

The movement within me that gives rise to this sharing is a movement that cares not if you agree or disagree, as there is no desire nor any interest in convincing you of anything. I do not count myself as an expert in any field, nor do I see myself as the authority in anyone's life other than my own. I say such things so there is a clear understanding that what I share is not meant to be the answer you are looking for, is not meant to cure you of anything; its only purpose is to share insight and wisdom as expressed through the Heart of this that I am. What you do with it is up to you.

If you find it helpful, this is your own doing. If you find it condemnable, this also is your own doing. All that is happening between you and I is a sharing of perspective, a sharing of insight and wisdom that may or may not ring true for your most sincere self. As I write, I write only to the One I Am.

Chapters

Chapter 1
An Explosion of Love

An Explosion of Love is how I would describe the unfolding of an Awakened Heart. As the mind quiets its quest to condemn, judge, and prove itself as right, it becomes clear that the voice in your Heart truly desires to bring well-being to all areas of your life.

This "well-being," can be seen as Love's Explosion; it can also be seen as the focus of this book, along with a more clear understanding of the obstacles which seem to keep this well-being at a distance. The deeper you explore into the nature of Reality...the nature of your most primary Self, what you discover is the Color of All Things Beautiful.

You notice that the life you once thought to be problematic and nauseating is actually a gift waiting to be opened and embraced. In this discovery, True Beauty emerges. What was once seen to be a curse, quite clearly becomes the lessons in Love you have craved so sincerely. Consequently, you give up the fight within your being that wants to be better, that wants to change the self with the hope of becoming more whole, and you enter into a space which for now can only be characterized as profoundly beautiful, unimaginably peaceful, and empty of any doubt, confusion, and fear.

For the one who cannot see this beauty, I would suggest that deep down you *know* it's there; even if you've turned away from the possibility that you might one day make love to its presence. Instinctively you know something calls to you, knowing that wellness exists somewhere, which of course is why you look for it. You search for it amidst your three dimensional world as a child searches for their favorite and most beloved toy. Because you can't find it, because you feel separate from it, your heart hurts as it longs to reunite with a Love that seems lost.

This of course is the life of most human beings, constantly caught up in a search for something that cannot be named; finding defeat around every corner as a loneliness is discovered in every experience that you thought would bring you home.

You see the battle wounds of this journey as it manifests itself in the form of soulful dis-ease and a physical body that simply feels drained, robotic, and insufficient. Simply put, you feel separate from all of life around you; as if you've fallen into a deep void that has imprisoned your heart and made living life a journey to be feared, rather than a joyful experience to be embraced and loved.

> *What was once seen to be a curse, quite clearly becomes the lessons in Love you have craved so sincerely.*

So, where-in lies the Freedom, the Liberation? Would it be too simple to suggest its presence is within you right now?

For most, yes, it would be an insult to suggest such simplicity, or to insinuate that it's here and you're simply not seeing it. However, yes, this is what I am suggesting. The answer or solution that's been looked for, searched for your entire life is actually with you right now in this very moment.

The solution or remedy to all your conflict, drama, and soulful dis-ease is not something that you will find in a tomorrow, but rather this gift is something you have been with your entire life. It is as if you were a flower who waits for permission to bloom, not realizing the permission has already been granted.

For the one who is offended by such a statement, I say that it is your insistence on being offended that blinds you to the Freedom staring right at you this very moment. Open up and realize that maybe, just maybe, it is this simple.

If you complicate your Blooming into this Love with the mind's judgments, rather than simply allowing yourself to remain open to the unknown, you will never see it for what it is nor can it be experienced. If you believe so strongly that this Love is beyond the most simple of things, you will create a life experience that proves your belief to be correct; living a life where Love is always at a distance.

When you see this depth in Life that is pointed to in this book, this ever-present something that desires only to support you, one of your first questions will be.... "How could I have ever missed this?"

Therefore, I encourage you to not turn this into a journey that requires struggle or personal will, but rather let Life show you the simplest of things... which is your most Natural state, and your most Primary Self; the Self that exists before conflict and drama arise.

There is nothing for you to learn, memorize, or adhere to, but rather there is only the embodiment of what you already are. And to hear this call, you must be willing to forget everything you think you know, and intimately know... that which comes *before* everything. You must be willing to lay down your judgments, your opinions, and all your efforts to prove yourself as right. If you carry with you a refusal to lay down the content in the mind, this discovery is only going to irritate you.

There is a reason why much of your internal explosions of Love are spawned through heartache. And the reason is, they are discovered only after you have given up on the mind's quest to solve problems through dualistic thinking. You accept fully that you don't really know, and in this stillness you become open for Life to show the way. This of course is why humility has been touted by mystics, spiritual teachers, and sages as being a bridge to Awakening.

The challenge here for most is that you have become so accustomed to current dogmas and beliefs that you use them to define who you *think* you are, and the thought of setting the beliefs aside is seen as a threat to your identity, so it hurts and is often met with plenty of resistance and defensiveness.

If you get defensive or irritated while reading any of this, that is a perfect example of how you feel threatened when someone suggests something that is not in alignment with what you believe so strongly. Be of good cheers though, because this is one of those little gifts trying to show you the damage being created by holding onto content in the mind.

No one is asking you to agree with anything being stated; on the contrary I ask that you leave agreement and disagreement out of it, and rather open your Heart to be touched by something deeper than words, deeper than opinion, and deeper than ideologies.

The words I use, as far as I'm concerned mean absolutely nothing, nor do I see them as being absolutely True. The purpose of this expression is not to convince you of anything, but rather to create a space for your own depth to be discovered with more clarity, more sincerity, which has nothing to do with words.

It is an easy trap to get caught up in, to become distracted by the words being used and then use your arguments to reinforce why the words I use are wrong, or invalid. To do this is to completely miss the point, even though it is a common movement of the mind to do such a thing. To argue about the words I choose to use is like arguing over the proper description of a color. If I say the sky is blue, you might argue that really it is more of a baby blue, or turquoise blue, missing the point entirely that I'm simply pointing to how beautifully blue the sky is.

If you argue about color or description, you quite sincerely miss the message; you miss the point of it all. If you are determined to be right in your way of seeing color, or Life, then you close yourself off to the real beauty in the colors, or in Life.

Silly humans we are, arguing about what name shall define God, cherishing the labels and defending mental content that exists only as a dream in the mind. All the while you miss the breath that gives Life to you, you miss the touch of silence, you miss the splendor of this moment. You want to argue about what to call the trees, or the mountains, missing the Reality that you are not separate from these happenings as they are an extension of your most primary Self, they are your most beautiful creation.

This points to the major challenge in Awakening to such a profound Love. In your effort to argue with what is, and to resist the moment as it arises, you perpetuate an effort to hold onto your old ways of seeing life. If at any time you argue with Reality by saying what IS should not be, you are quite sincerely turning away from the hand of Life that desires for you to be well and filled with Love. "How could this be?," you ask. Well, stick around Dear One, for this discovery awaits to unfold.

Who am I to say such things? What authority do I have to address matters of your most intimate Self? Please understand that the relevance of me has no relevance at all. As with all your other beliefs, I ask that you also lay down your beliefs about who you *think* I am. This Awakening within you will have nothing to do with me, and everything to do with your own willingness to see clearly. The profound insight you may receive from these teachings are in fact your own creation; for you are the one who interprets, the one who is willing, and the one who holds the power to Awaken to the Love within yourself.

I fully release any desire or expectation within me that wants you to do anything, or be other than as you are right now, for the only thing I wish upon you is complete Freedom.

This is a delicate unfolding, and because it is as such, I encourage you to move with caution. Let us not rush through the content in this book. I encourage you to take your time and allow the content to be your friend rather than trying to determine whether or not it is right or wrong.

> *If at any time you argue with Reality, by saying what is should not be, you are quite sincerely turning away from the hand of Life that desires for you to be well and filled with Love.*

One of the major difficulties in allowing this wisdom to penetrate your Heart is your quest to determine my intent, or hanging onto assumptions about what I am saying or what I am not saying. If you find yourself to be caught up in such a thing, what you see is not the wisdom that wants to shine through but rather only your judgments.

As you read this book, or engage in its content, let us not be consumed with a quest to determine the author's validity, but only look to see if the content or insight resonates within your being. The tone that carries my desire to write this book is one of dispassionate compassion; meaning, I care deeply for the well-being of humankind, however, I do not desire to find myself caught up in the delusions of the drama and suffering that you may experience.

I understand that the suffering you live with may seem very real and valid, and at times it may seem as though I discredit your suffering. However, what is really happening is that the content in this book is challenging your perception. If one is not ready to discover this deeper Love, these challenges will only be seen as threats.

If you find yourself being threatened, which is only an expression of suffering, let us not blame the content or author, but rather look within ourselves and ask, "How is it that I can experience internal dis-ease from simply reading words on a piece of paper, and why is it I feel compelled to blame something external as the cause of how I feel internally?"

Such questions will lead to an Awakening that will allow you to live life unhindered by the external world, which means you can engage life and not feel threatened by that which is outside you. Such a thing may seem like an impossibility, but then again that is why you are here in this moment with this book in your hand. Something deep within you knows there is an internal gift that together we can described as liberation from suffering.

From my perception, it seems like an impossibility that someone could read this book with a willing Heart and not extract some wisdom that will most definitely lead to a life lived with more Love and less fear. Of course, if you read this book only with an intent to criticize it, or to discover how it is in someway wrong or invalid, I assure you this will be your discovery.

> *Why is it I feel compelled to blame something external as the cause of how I feel internally?"*

Chapter 2
Fear

Fear has become a hindrance to your Awakening because you cling to it as if it's your worst enemy.

Most people live their lives with a sole effort to avoid fear; to run from that which seems to threaten their well being. So... how's that working so far?

To address this movement of fear, I'll say directly that fear is a result of feeling as though there is something to be lost; the greater the perceived loss, the more intense the feeling of fear will be. What I invite you to discover, in our time together, is the profound realization that there is nothing for you to lose, even though your mind emphatically believes otherwise.

Quite often I find myself hiking in the beautiful Southern Oregon Valley and one of my favorite locations to hike in the valley is a place called Lower Table Rock. At the trail-head there are several warning signs to keep a sharp eye out for rattlesnakes. In my numerous excursions on this trail, I've seen five rattlesnakes as well as a number of other snakes that keep company with a diverse range of lizards, caterpillars, squirrels, deer, and the occasional coyote.

On this particular trip that I'm referring to, I had the idea of snakes on my mind. Since I've almost stepped on a baby rattlesnake before, I am accustomed to watching where I place my feet. As I was making my way up this beautiful path, I was gripped momentarily by fear as I saw at my feet what appeared to be a large brown spotted snake.

At this moment I felt a surge of adrenaline that was preparing my body to move with quickness. As I became fully aware of the sensation in my body, a curious thing happened as I looked more closely. What I discovered with great clarity is that what I was afraid of was not a snake that may bite, but rather a harmless little stick! Yes, I broke out with joyful laughter.

What happened here is that my mind perceived something that wasn't real, based on past conditioning and where my attention was. So what I was actually afraid of was only a dream in my mind, a fabrication of my imagination. It didn't matter that it was a dream, my mind still responded as though it was real, simply because of the fact that I perceived it as real.

> *Fear is a result of feeling as though there is something to be lost; the greater the perceived loss, the more intense the feeling of fear will be.*

I will also note that the snake didn't cause the fear even if it was real; the fear was caused by my perception, by the story being told in my mind about what I was seeing.

Here is the part I find so interesting... What is the knee jerk reaction of most human beings when they encounter something they believe is fearful? The most common response is to turn and run away, not simply to turn and walk, but to turn and *run*. There is zero interest in the investigation of the fear, but only an attempt to run and find something that is not fearful.

Let's slow down here and cover a quick point that will shed light on this delusion. Remember, I mentioned that fear is a response to the belief or perception that something can and will be lost. Well, this *something* that you are trying to protect, so adamantly, is none other than your perceived identity. You believe that you will lose some element of what you are and therefore respond with fear so as to protect who or what you are thought to be.

Let's look at it this way; you come to Earth as a human being, and one of your gifts to function and survive is this element called fear. In the face of danger, this survival fear initiates a response within your being to make it known quite abruptly that you are about to lose your life. This is very helpful in a situation where a car might be just moments away from striking you. However, this sensation of fear to protect your physical life is a little different from the fear most people deal with on a day-to-day basis.

Most people's experience of fear consists of a movement that seems to squeeze the joy from Life. It seems to hijack your well-being and bind you to a prison that exists in your mind. You become terribly anxious, stressed out, depressed, heartbroken and the like. Part of the delusion that makes this fearful existence so painful is that the fear you feel internally is usually attributed to some external circumstance.

Remember the example of the imaginary snake? It wasn't the stick or snake itself that was scary, but rather my perception of what I stood to lose in the story I told myself about the event. The event itself was empty of fear as the whole dilemma was created in my mind.

Look closely at this Dear One; it is not the events in your life that create fear or the lack of love you experience, but rather it is your *perception* of those events that create the internal response of dis-ease. Can you see the vicious cycle that is created by believing the cause of fear exists outside what you are? This gives rise to your incessant blaming by believing that other people are responsible for your suffering. In this cycle there is no way out as you will never find a solution to your suffering in the external world because it is not the external world that creates it.

For some, hearing such things creates a wonderful sense of Freedom by knowing the solution resides within what 'one is' rather than in the external world. It is at this point of discovery that you can take responsibility for your life experience and allow for change to unfold. However, for others, hearing this only creates more anger, as they feel that their condemnation of the outside world is being threatened, and there lies a possibility that they are wrong.

I assure you, this has nothing to do with being right or wrong, but has everything to do with your own experience of Liberation and Love. Again, I'm not trying to convince you of anything, I'm simply pointing out some insight that might help you see more clearly into the source of your suffering.

But since I brought it up, let's look at this example of someone getting angry over what I've just said. Like I mentioned already, fear or anger are emotional responses to the perception that you are going to lose your identity, your worth, or who it is you think you are. When fear arises in this scenario it is because you have attached your identity to your beliefs. So when your beliefs are threatened or challenged, it is taken personally, as if *you* are being threatened, and therefore the body responds with fear; in this case it may manifest as anger.

Is it True though? Is it the Truth that what you believe determines your worth, value, or identity? Is it True that the content floating through your mind somehow defines who or what you are?

If I believe a tree to be a special tree, does it really make it special, or does it simply remain as it always has, regardless of my thoughts about it?

If I believe a flower to be small, does it actually mean that it's small, or does it merely point to a comparison being made that's not based on Truth, but rather is based on what I compare it to? Quite simply this same flower could be large if compared to a smaller flower; such comments from the mind have nothing to do with the actual flower, but only refer to my experience or how I choose to perceive it. Independent of my perception, the flower remains as it always has been.

> *It is not the events in your life that create fear or the lack of love you experience, but rather it is your perception of those events that create the internal response of dis-ease.*

Referring back to the example of the angry student who probably isn't reading this book anymore, what you are afraid of or angry with are not my comments, but your own perception, which says that what you believe defines who you are. This is the process of every heated argument, which is the attempt to protect your identity by protecting your opinions, beliefs, and ideas.

Surely you can see that what is being protected is only imaginary. It is a stick that is believed to be a snake. The anger that ensues is a form of running from fear, and what is being run from exists only as a dream in the mind. It's referred to as "running" when you aren't willing to **STOP** and investigate. You respond with a knee jerk reaction as you believe the fear to be real and you will do whatever you can to survive, which is to get angry with the hope that you can prove your belief as the right belief, validating who it is you *think* you are.

All of your running from fear, whether you realize it or not, is really running from nothing. You are running from a dream in the mind, a story that threatens what you cling to for identity.

Herein lays the call for quiet meditative listening. The robotic life most people live out is one of fear filled conditioning with responses that are completely unconscious. The good news is that as you become more aware of this delusion, or mistaken perception, the force that ties you to the dream world loosens and you begin to experience life with more Ease, Beauty and Love.

Knowing that fear is a creation that takes place within yourself, you might find yourself more willing to look at it, rather than run from it. It's easy to run if you believe the cause of fear to be external, since the moment it arises you *think* you don't have to take responsibility for it as it is believed to be beyond you. If the cause of fear is recognized as an internal happening, then you might notice that running from it is an impossibility. It is like trying to run away from your feet.

> *This is the process of every heated argument, which is the attempt to protect your identity by protecting your opinions, beliefs, and ideas.*

It doesn't help much that for thousands of years people have been conditioned to believe that fear exists outside of oneself, in the form of a devil or persons whose only goal is to keep them from wellness. If you can convince someone that their problems are caused by something external, then you can create a solution that they can run to. This is similar to what can be seen in social power systems (politics/government/religion); create a problem and then create a solution that reinforces the external savior's validity.

This isn't to say the external devil path is irrelevant; I'm just pointing to the possibility that perhaps it's time to deal with your own suffering, rather than looking to something external to bring liberation to your Soul.

For some, such a path of religious dogma might be helpful, but if you're reading *this* book then I'm assuming that within you is an Awareness that knows Life exists on a deeper level; rather than believing in a story where people literally burn up for all of eternity if their beliefs and moral conduct are not in alignment with someone else's interpretation of texts written thousands of years ago and transcribed numerous times.

Written words are not meant to be used as the source of discovery for Truth, but are rather meant to be used as signposts that might or might not point in the direction of your most Profound Unfolding. The delusion, though, is that these words and their stories have been used to define who we are rather than using them as pointers to discover That which is beyond words. Consequently, we have killed each other over the protection of these words and beliefs, simply because we believe they define us... Silly humans.

Let this be a profound starting point, the deep acknowledgment that the experience of fear is not a result of anything external, but rather a result of perception; of how we see out into the world from behind our eyes.

Chapter 3
Awakening

Before we get too lost in words, let's clarify this concept of *Awakening*. As I mentioned earlier, words are used as pointers and tools to assist you in your life discovery. Words themselves mean nothing other than the meaning you give them.

For example, if I were to say "Large," your mind creates a story about what "large" means based on your experience, but the word itself can't actually define something. A cup isn't large, or small, it is as it is. To say it is Large is to compare it to another cup; without the comparison, the cup is neither large nor small.

If you look at a coffee cup and think... "that cup is small," can you see how this exposes your environmental conditioning where you have grown up with cups that appear larger in size.

For the one who grew up with tiny cups, your coffee cup to them is actually quite large. Who is right?

For one person the word "Awakening" could mean 'something wonderful,' but for someone else the same word could mean 'something from the devil.' Do you see this clearly?

Which one is right, or true, 'something wonderful' or 'something from the devil?'

Your Meaning, or the Story being told in your mind about what this word means, isn't really true, but rather it just exposes your conditioning.

There are a million different interpretations you could give to this word "awakening," and the interpretation that you give will determine how you dance with it.

Awakening, in the sense that I use the word, merely points to what happens as you begin to see life with more clarity or more accurately. You could debate to no end on what it means to see life clearly or accurately, however, I have no interest in debating, since to debate, one must use words, and words never accurately describe anything; what is being pointed to in this book, quite sincerely, is *beyond* words.

There is nothing within me that says you must resonate with these words, nor is there any condemnation for not understanding what I speak of. Using the example of attempting to speak to you in a foreign language, just because it makes sense to me, in no way it means you will understand it. I encourage you to release any frustration that might arise from any confusion you experience, for this frustration only deepens the difficulty.

Simply allow the natural flow; take what feels true and leave what does not. Stand on your own authority and trust the movement within yourself.

The concept of Awakening can also be referred to as Being Awake, and our life before Awakening can be referred to as living asleep.

Living as an asleep human being refers to living as if the dream in our mind is real; believing that words and mental constructs actually define what is being observed. An example of this is living as though your judgments about other people are actually true and you treat them and yourself as such. When you live this way, asleep, you set yourself up for suffering and as you Awaken, your suffering becomes less, as Love explodes within your entire life experience.

Another example of asleep living is believing that other people's thoughts about you define who you are, and therefore, you live with the intent of manipulating people's opinions of you. You live life trying to get others to see you in a certain way, with the hope that it will make you more of what you long for... Wholeness. This movement is a recipe for internal dis-ease as it sets you up on a quest that goes nowhere, other than maybe showing you that it doesn't work.

There is a natural movement in life to bring you to a place of Awakening, to see life more clearly. This is the purpose of suffering. When you suffer, it's as if an alarm goes off within you that says you are not seeing Reality as it is, you are clinging to an illusion. Just as physical pain shows you something in your body is out of whack, inner suffering or dis-ease points to an "out of sync" way of living, or perceiving.

> *When you suffer, it's as if an alarm goes off within you that says you are not seeing Reality as it is, you are clinging to an illusion.*

The challenge, for most people, is that they run from this suffering as if it doesn't have a right to be, but in Truth it serves a great purpose as a wake-up call. However, if you run from suffering, you'll never see the lesson that is trying to present itself.

It also might be important to touch here upon the concept of "Enlightenment," which points to living life in a fully Awakened state. However, please be clear about this, the concept of *Enlightenment* is only a pointer and not an end result. So I encourage you not to turn *Enlightenment* into some sort of goal or prize; simply allow it to point to an ever-deepening clarity.

I hesitate to even use this word, enlightenment, because I've seen it used in so many other ways that are not in alignment with its ancient meaning. In today's culture, the word is commonly interpreted as gaining in some type of worldly mind knowledge, having nothing to do with the truth of Reality as a Whole.

These words, *Enlightenment* and *Awakening*, have an ancient history and both point to a similar experience of seeing reality with more clarity. In the Christian tradition, the pointer is being *Born Again*, or *Saved*. In all honesty though, this term of being Born Again has been perverted and associated with adopting a belief structure or dogma, which has nothing to do with Truth or clear perception.

Of course, the same error can be associated with the terms *Awakening* and *Enlightenment* as well, which happens quite often. This is why I stress the point of not holding onto such labels, lest you become lost in your own mental noise and start believing your label as the right label.

Here is a quote from my other book, *Intimacy With the Silent Nothing that is Everything*, that I think helps to clarify the subject of living Awake.

Living life as a human who is asleep,
is like trying to build a tower with tiny bricks,
while sitting in the middle of the freeway.
Your tower is constantly knocked over by passing motorist,
while you are determined to keep building.
Living life as an Awake human,
is realizing there is no brick;
and you wonder what the hell you're doing in the middle of
the freeway.

In this passage I point to how living asleep is similar to building a collection of thought with the hope it might define you, or create Wholeness in your life. When you wake up, you realize that wellness cannot be found in the mind through attaching yourself to labels and concepts. You realize how silly such a thing is to find yourself in a dream... and the whole process becomes quite hilarious!

As you begin to Awaken, or begin to see Life with more clarity, often it can become quite disorienting. You realize your whole life has been based on something that isn't even real; you have been serving a dream rather than serving the Life that's right before you.

I feel it is necessary to take time to clarify what it is we are Awakening from. We've touched a little bit on this concept of the dream, but let's go further.

The world you experience is determined by perception, or how you perceive what is being observed. Just as if you see a ladybug, you can see this tiny creature as a threat or a beautiful expression of Life, or maybe even as a friend. How you perceive it, how you see it, will greatly influence your experience with it.

If the ladybug is seen as a threat, try and visualize how you might respond. Maybe you cringe, or withdraw yourself from its Presence; it is even possible that you may smash the insect and take its life. Remember, it's not actually the ladybug's fault that you feel threatened, but rather it is how you see the ladybug that creates your response.

You can even see how conditioning plays out here. As a child you might have been around someone who hated ladybugs and you simply adopted their perception. This, of course, points to where and how we construct our mental patterns through our environment.

Your interaction with life begins with how you see life; most people truly believe that how they see life is a reflection of how life really is. This naturally points to our collective insanity in passionately trying to convince others that they are wrong, when in Truth, it's not an issue of right and wrong.

Do you notice within yourself this movement that I'm referring to, the times when you become disgusted with the worldview or opinion of someone else? Your disgust is not based on what is True, but rather is based on your effort to support your own world view or opinion in the hope that you can reaffirm who it is you *think* you are.

You get disgusted internally because you want to reinforce how *you* see life, and proclaim that it is the *right* way to see life. The Truth of the matter is you have the freedom to perceive however you see fit *and* so does everyone else. To not give others this same freedom, means you delude yourself even further into an asleep way of living by clinging to your own thoughts, which makes you a prisoner to your own mind.

As you Awaken, you naturally give others the freedom to live out their existence, and in giving this freedom, you find it much easier to let go of the limiting thoughts in your mind.

What you are Awakening from, is your false perception, your dream. If you desire this Awakening, you must see clearly that what exists in the mind is not Reality but only the imagination at play. Reality or Truth refers to what is Real, and what is real can only exist in this moment. You are waking up to this Reality and letting go of the dream; do you see the simplicity here?

> **Reality or Truth refers to what is Real, and what is real can only exists in this moment.**

Please don't complicate it or turn it into something mystical. The mind wants to turn this into some sort of a problem to solve, by making it more complicated than what it really is; this is the mind looking for a reward of sorts so it can feel right, victorious or validated.

It's easy to ask the question, "If it's so simple then how come everyone is not Awake?" Allow me to ask a follow up question, "If a fish looks for water, how long will it take before it is successful?" You are searching for Wholeness, looking for that something which will make you well again but the answer is right in front of you. You are literally breathing the solution as you look for it, so the simple act of looking for it means you don't know that it's right in front of you.

It's much like looking for your sunglasses as they softly sit on your forehead. However, if you were to be still, and stop looking for something outside yourself, you would notice the solution has been within you the whole time.

Often this Awakening unfolds after a deeply painful life experience, a deep suffering that brings you to your knees. This is because you give up trying; you give up looking for something outside yourself, while ending the search and simply admitting that you do not know.

Has this not been your experience, in which out of heartache comes a deeper connection with Life? Such profound growth stems from such experiences, and it's simply because you are humbled, you are shown that the mind does not know.

The difficulty in this unfolding is not the Awakening itself, but the resistance leading up to Awakening. Just as when heartache leads towards growth, the heartache is a result of your resistance toward what wants to be seen. The actual breakthrough is simple; the less you resist the lessons wanting to be shown, the faster you learn the lesson and experience a new depth in Life.

The path towards Awakening is best served when you stop fighting with Life, when you stop arguing with Reality. As you see with more clarity that Life wants to support you, you naturally loosen your grip on the thoughts that are in opposition to whatever is appearing in any given moment. You alone will be the one who gives yourself permission to let go of the battle that rages in your mind.

Seeing Reality as an Awake Being is an absolute breath of fresh air. As described here in this passage from my previously referenced book....

You know that sigh of relief that comes with waking up from a nightmare?

The sensation that follows the realization - "oh my god, it was only a dream."

All of a sudden one realizes there is nothing to fear, for what we were afraid of losing wasn't even real.

My friend, this is the overwhelming sensation of peace that awaits all who perceive Truth.

As described by numerous mystics, sages, and true spiritual teachers of the past and the present, what is recognized is an overwhelming sensation that... All is incredibly well. Not because we psych ourselves out and repeat positive affirmations, but because it *is* the Truth of Reality.

I understand fully, that to the asleep being such a thing sounds ridiculous and far-fetched, but again I'm not here to convince you of the goodness that is available in this moment, this is simply an invitation to discover within yourself a deeper connection with the Life that you are.

> *The difficulty in this unfolding is not the Awakening itself, but the resistance leading up to Awakening.*

Chapter 4
The Quest for Identity

Whether you are aware of it or not, what takes up the vast majority of your energy and resources is the quest to discover or solidify who you are. This may unfold in numerous ways such as looking for the perfect educational degree, in relationships with others, or in the purchase of items that you want to define you. The avenues to reach such an end result are endless or infinite.

If you have lived for any length of time in this experience called life, you have probably learned that manipulating the external world, to get what you want, is not a recipe for internal well-being. Time and time again you learn that getting what you want often leads towards disappointment as the internal void creeps up like a stranger you can't run away from.

Even though you know that getting what you want won't satisfy your Soul, you continue the quest of seeking for satisfaction outside yourself. You continue on a path that is hell bent on achieving, succeeding, and acquiring that which you hope will relieve the discontent you've become accustomed to. This cycle will repeat itself until death without liberation if you are unwilling to get honest and question your intent and your identity.

Much of the difficulty is in simply not understanding, or the lack of awareness into what is actually going on. Once you see with great clarity the inner workings of these movements called seeking, quite naturally you will see the seeking fall away with little to no effort on your part.

To put it simply, the quest for identity is an attempt to discover who or what you are. In other words, it is your effort to solidify the Self and know with certainty the validity of your existence.

This is a natural pull of Life, a natural yearning that everyone experiences; and to be very direct, regardless of what you think you want in life, this quest of Self-discovery is the driving force of your being. When the realization of what you are hits you deeply, all suffering and conflict drops away and no longer becomes a problem in your life. Of course, what spawns the search is the suffering you experience. Instinctively, you know suffering to be out of alignment with the natural and unrestricted flow of Life, so you look for wellness.

The challenge, of course, is that you look for it in all the wrong places and the discovery seems to be elusive. What keeps you so distant from this unfolding of Awakening is that you look for Self where Self is not present. You look for it in the acquisition of things, in people, in mental concepts and the like; the moment you think you've found it, somehow it floats away.

> *Once you see with great clarity the inner workings of these movements called seeking, quite naturally you will see the seeking fall away with little to no effort on your part.*

One element that is required to see your depth is a deep acceptance and acknowledgment that what you are looking for cannot be found in the external world, or in the mind. If you aren't ready to accept this, you are encouraged to keep trying external seeking until you simply realize for yourself that it is not working. Again, I'm not asking you to accept it because I'm telling you to; I'm asking that you look at your own experience and question. Question the life you've lived and simply be honest with yourself. Give attention to all the things you've chased with the hope it would bring about peace and well-being, as well as all your efforts to reduce suffering, etc.

Most people have simply experienced suffering moving around within their experience from relationships to finances, from finances to health, from health back to relationships again. Suffering has become a cycle that doesn't truly dissolve, it merely hides and re-emerges.

In these writings, I'm pointing to a Freedom where one Awakens from the game of suffering permanently. I am pointing to a direct path of discovery, where you get honest with yourself, and stop chasing that which can never provide sustenance. In the end of seeking, you discover a Wholeness that has always been present and will never leave. Yes, such a thing does sound lovely. But...There is a reason why Awakening seems to happen only for a few; this is because of the "death" one must go through in order to discover their True Self.

> *I am pointing to a direct path of discovery, where you get honest with yourself, and stop chasing that which can never provide sustenance.*

To clarify the teachings we've heard over the past two thousand years and beyond; this space of Awakening has been referred to as Heaven. Before you get all hot and bothered about using Christian terminology, remember that these teachings originally were meant to be used as pointers. The truly Enlightened Ones who first taught these lessons had no intent for the teachings to be hijacked and turned into an exclusive club only for those who did what they were commanded to do.

The actual "event" of Awakening, Enlightenment, or being Born Again, has nothing to do with a choice you make, or an external *event*. It is an internal opening that happens through the surrender of your Being, through a recognition of something that cannot be spoken or written about; something that is much deeper than anything that is produced from the mind.

Since this movement of Truth is experienced *beyond* the surface, manifesting in a multitude of ways, there is diversity in spiritual teachings and teachers, all of which are neither right nor wrong. They simply are as they are, and you, through your perception, determine their validity based on your own experience as a human being. Any effort to judge one teaching or path, in comparison with another, is not to truly define it, but is to proclaim your own conditioning and life experience as better than the rest.

This idea of Heaven has been described as an amazing space of Love, Peace, and Beauty; with suffering being an old and tired experience that's not permitted beyond the pearly gates. Remember, how I mentioned that this discovery of Awakening is beyond words, beyond stories, and ideas? Well then, how can you describe something that is beyond description? You can't... you simply do what you can to point to it, and the descriptions you've heard in the past do just that.

When you see the depth of the Truth within yourself, when you Awaken, the life experience is characterized as something that is of the highest Love, the most profound Beauty, and the deepest Peace imaginable. Be careful though as your *idea* of Love may not be the kind of Love that is being referred to. If your idea of Love comes with external conditions, which means you get what you want; then you are setting yourself up for a major disappointment.

The experience of this Love, Beauty, and Peace is completely an inside job; it is an experience that happens within what you are. Yes, it is true that your physical experience might dramatically change; meaning you live with more ease and the Whole of Life seems as if its sole intent is to support you. But if you go into it with expectations of how it should be or should not be, you have already set yourself up to not see your deepest nature.

I might as well address the concept of hell and point to its experience as being full of suffering. The images that have been used to describe hell, again, aren't to define it, but are meant to point to something deeper. You have probably had the internal experience in which you feel like you are living a very real hell. This might take the shape of being emotionally paralyzed to the point of vomiting, or maybe you have found yourself to be drowning with insecurities that bind you, and keep you from following the Heart's calling.

What is being pointed to with the term "hell," is a massive restriction of Love. In this restriction of Love, your experience as a human being becomes unpleasant and unnatural. As you live bound to stress, anxiety, heartache and the like; you are experiencing the hell that's been pointed to for thousands of years. The liberation that awaits is your Awakening from this dream of hell, as you enter into this space that is referred to as Heaven.

All of these authentic teachings that you've seen passed down through the generations are meant to serve you in *this* Life; the life that is happening now, **right now**. It is not meant to prepare you for some event in the future, and therefore, to cling to these teachings with the belief that it will protect you from some future apocalypse is to completely miss the point of the profound Truth that waits to be discovered in this moment.

What is this business of death happening before Heaven can be experienced, as it's been referred to in past teachings? To say it directly, this is a metaphorical death that happens while you are present in each moment. It is a dying to a self that is not real, and embodying a Self that *is* real. Also, you can call it a letting go, or surrendering, which is a movement that stops trying to control life and becomes One with Life.

This topic of dying to a false self will be covered thoroughly in the coming chapters. To touch on it briefly, I'll say that this death is the beginning of a new Life. It is waking up from a life that has been lived asleep, and upon your Awakening you sincerely experience what seems to be a new Life.

I suggest not turning Awakening into a goal, as a goal implies that something is going to happen tomorrow or some other time than now. I assure you, the only space where Awakening will unfold is *now*. By default, if you perceive Awakening, or your True Self as something to be discovered tomorrow; you project it away from you and create distance by believing it is not available in this moment. This, of course, is part of the delusion that makes it seem so inaccessible, the idea that it's not already here and simply waiting to be seen.

What you are truly searching for is a connection, a reunion of Heart, Soul, and Being; a return to the Heaven from which you came. The search is for the Truth of what you are, and when discovered, a new world emerges; a world you never knew existed and only heard stories of.

One of the major difficulties people have is trying to understand how a new world can emerge, or how you can seemingly be transported to a place that's full of Love, Beauty and Peace although it appears that there is so much devastation, heartache, corruption, etc. in the world. Well, for now all I can say is keep reading.

Chapter 5
Time

I am going to ask you to take time to visualize something with me.

Imagine you are floating in outer space a billion miles from the sun. It's just you all alone with no cell phone, no clock, nor gadgets of any kind, and naked. Even though you are not standing on the planet earth, and there exists no gravity, you are still very much Present and Alive. All that you experience is space, and a Present Awareness that knows of its own existence.

Really feel this.

Feel what it would be like to have no sound, no rising of the sun, no sunset, nothing in front of you and nothing behind you; just space, simply existing and Being. As you spend your moments here just floating in nothing, you fall asleep. When your eyes open, you ask... "How much time have I spent sleeping?" Well, if you were on earth, you might check your watch, or look to the position of the sun to determine an approximate amount of time. You might even close your eyes and think real hard, but the important question here is will you ever know how long you slept without an external reference like the sun or a watch?

Even better, how long would you have to be in this part of the universe before you completely lose all concept of time?

What's the value of such an exercise? Well, hopefully you see that what I'm pointing to is that "time" is not a reality, but rather a creation of the human mind. It is a tool used to better communicate with each other while living out this seemingly three dimensional linear experience.

There is a pattern of how planet Earth circles the sun, and since it is consistent; it can be used as a measuring tool to help us function. In the beginning it may have been said, "Meet me in the desert when the sun is directly above you." Now it's called high noon, or twelve o'clock. Is it true though? Is it true there exists something that's called "twelve o'clock?" Or is it merely making reference to something that's not real, but rather an idea that helps us to communicate?

Much like if I point to "Southern Oregon" on a map of the United States; it doesn't mean that I'm actually pointing to my current place of residence. It just makes reference to help you understand the location. Even if the name United States is used, it doesn't make reference to something that is real; it only points to an idea that many have mistakenly claimed as real.

If you believe such things as the "United States" to be real and true, you end up doing what many have done and experience suffering through the attempt to protect a label or ideal that isn't even here now. It can be quite a shock for some to discover that those things that are *believed* to be real, are actually dreams playing out in the human mind.

Let's get back to this space of Eternity; as you return to your meditative place in the outer reaches of the Universe surrounded only by space. As you are here, floating in nothing, ask yourself... "What is Real?" Not... "What do I *believe, think*, or *hope* is real, but what is *actually* real?

The difference between what *actually is* Real and the dream is quite clear; your years of conditioning have convinced you of the dream being real, so initially it will require a willingness on your part to investigate the nature of Reality and the nature of the dream world. The wonderful news though is that what is Real is really Real and never *not* Real; what is a dream, comes and goes and is a product of the mind's imagination.

Living and breathing what *is* Real is the new life being stepped into rather than living in service to a dream that is only *thought* to be real. So in this quiet space ask, "What is Real?

When the question... "What is True?" takes precedent over... "What do I want?" you will surely discover your most intimate nature and fall with Grace into open arms of complete Love.

In this space that has no time, since time isn't Real, is the space we call Eternity; it is Now, it is This Moment. Because you have been convinced that time is an actuality, you look at the word Eternity and believe it to be something linear that goes on in a straight line like time. Maybe you see it as a straight line that has no end. The profound Truth, though, is that there is no line.

It might help to see your self in this meditative space with no reference point, and ask yourself, "What is up, and what is down?" With nothing to reference, there is no up and there is no down. Without getting into the science of all, which is irrelevant to seeing your most primary Self, this moment is Eternity. The concept of Eternity points to a depth in Life; it does not point to a linear concept of time.

Infinity takes place Now, not tomorrow, and in this Now is everything you need to be the complete and whole Self you have always been.

One of the reasons this whole idea of Eternity or Infinity is so elusive is simply because it's beyond the mind's ability to contemplate. You can't pin it down by thinking about it, and every time you try, it becomes a mystery again. The profound Truth here is to see clearly that the nature of Reality, the nature of Truth is Infinite and

Eternal. You will never be able to comprehend its existence with the mind; you cannot count to Infinity nor can you count to your own depth.

Other points of confusion are in the old teachings of religion in which the concept is that people die and then pass on to Eternity and either suffer or have peace for all time. Even some translations say, "everlasting life," which implies there is some sort of time involved. As I mentioned earlier, Eternity has nothing to do with time, but has everything to do with this Moment, for this Moment is Eternal.

> *When the question... "What is True?" takes precedent over... "What do I want?" you will surely discover your most intimate nature and fall with Grace into open arms of complete Love.*

What I am pointing to is an Eternity of Peace or Infinite Well-Being that is available right Now. The Kingdom of Heaven is to see clearly the depth of this Moment; to live in the Infinite Now and not the dream state that is bound by concepts of time, limitation, and separation. The Kingdom of Heaven is within You; The "You" that exists right Now: not the you in the future that has its shit together.

In general, human beings are in a hurry to get somewhere or to achieve something. You have been conditioned that something is coming to rescue you, that something is right around the corner that will take away your suffering. If I might quickly address this, I'd say that in Truth, you and only you are going to be the one that saves you from suffering. However, the "You," that's going to be the savior of your world, is not the "you" that you *think* you are.

The encouragement that past sages and mystics have given about the need to be vigilant or watchful, weren't making reference to something that's coming tomorrow, but they were pointing to the importance of this Moment. For you to Awaken, you must find yourself engaged in Reality in this Moment; for it is only in this Moment that you Awaken to your most Divine Self. Be Present and experience this Now.

Humankind has taken this wisdom and created another dream about how something outside of oneself would be the savior of their world. So stories are told of the second coming of Christ, when in Truth you are the Christ. *You* are the Divine awaiting to return. It is up to you and only you, but a deeper You... a sacred You.

Just look at how much you rely on the exterior world to take care of your emotional well-being. In relationships, there is the absurd belief that your partner is responsible for your poor attitude. In society, there is the belief that the government, banks, and the greed of others are responsible for your life experience of lack and limitation.

Can you see how dysfunctional the human race can be as it pertains to living out Truth? We are but babes of a species who have barely scratched the surface in this movement called Life. Yet, we pretend to be so confident, as if we really know what the hell we're doing. We want so desperately to be liked by others because we so adamantly don't like ourselves, and again look to other people for the solution.

Quite simply, and hear this, if you want to discover the depth of your True Self, or to Awaken in this Eternal Moment, you must be **willing** to not look to external factors for your Source of sustenance. An important clarification here.... I am not saying, "Don't look," to the external; I'm saying, "Be *willing* to not look." There is a monumental difference.

The difference? To "be willing" is an invitation to be aware of your seeking and clinging to the external if you're Present enough to notice it. If I commanded you to "not seek," then this could create self-condemnation as you cling to the silly belief that you're doing something you're not supposed to be doing.

The Truth is, you are free to do whatever you do, so even if you were not willing, you would still be whole and complete, you just wouldn't notice your wholeness if you are looking to the external to find it.

> *The Kingdom of Heaven is within You; The "You" that exists right Now, not the you in the future that has its shit together.*

When you look to the external for your Source of well-being, you're actually looking to projections in the mind. If you look at a new car to make you happy, you are looking to your thoughts about that car, not the car itself. The car alone is as it is, neither good nor bad, it simply is. The mind creates a story about how it will make you more whole, more acceptable, or loveable. You then look to the attainment of the car to prove your thoughts as True. Does it work? No, it fails every time.

Can you see this clearly? You look at a car, and have all these glorious thoughts about what it would mean for you to be seen driving that car; what it would mean in how you felt about yourself. You're obsessed with mental noise about you being accepted or rejected, having nothing to do with the car itself! Crazy.

> **When you look to the external for your Source of well-being, you're actually looking to projections in the mind.**

Another example is, if I see someone do a cool trick on a skateboard and I think, "Wow! He's so awesome." If there are elements of inadequacy within me, I may try and compensate by taking on the task of learning how to skateboard so I too can be seen, and see myself as "awesome."

Therefore, I struggle and get pissed off as I practice day and night to learn how to pull off a skateboard trick so I can be whole or... awesome. If the time ever does come that I accomplish my goal, the internal victory will be short lived. For a while I will try and show anyone I can of my new accomplishment, with the hope that they will have the same thoughts that I once had about another skateboarder.

I do this with great enthusiasm, as I mistakenly believe that other people's thoughts will determine my worth. When in truth, their thoughts mean nothing, I simply give myself permission to see myself as awesome because I now believe others think I'm awesome. That shit is crazy!

An example that hits even closer to home for myself, since skateboarding is something I have no interest in, is an experience I had with my middle daughter who is currently eleven years old. One thing I can do relatively well is draw with pencils. On this particular day, my daughter and I were sitting down at the kitchen table and she was watching me draw a portrait of someone. During this time, I could see the amazement in her eyes as I skillfully yet effortless created a masterpiece, which to her must have been one of the coolest things she had ever seen.

She then made it her mission to get a piece of paper and draw a portrait on her own. Her task only met with heartache, frustration, and disappointment, as she discovered her ability to draw was nowhere close to dads. Do you see what happened here?

In her mind she had "awesome" thoughts about what I could do, as she proclaimed that I was awesome because I could draw so well. She herself wanted to be awesome as well, and therefore she desperately wanted to draw a picture that was just as amazing, with the intent that she could experience that awesomeness as her own identity.

First of all, she created a hopeful outcome that held her well-being. There was the internal projection that said personal worth is determined by how well she did something. As she engaged the task, this projection was threatened as she discovered that within her wasn't the ability at this time to draw as well as dad. Because this projected identity was threatened, she sincerely felt that her own worth was being threatened, therefore, she responded with a fear that manifested as heartache, frustration, and disappointment... a manifestation of hell.

This experience proved to be a fantastic lesson as we were able to address the suffering and bring clarity to it. I expressed to her that I don't draw because I want to be good or better than; I draw because I enjoy the process. As I draw, it is a form of expression that allows for me to share Love. If I experience suffering as I attempt to draw, I simply wouldn't engage in it. Again, the only reason I would experience suffering is if I believed my worth was wrapped around my ability to draw well.

I encouraged her not to draw because she wanted to be good, but to draw simply because she enjoys it. By giving up this idea that you have to be something that simply isn't there, you give up the idea that says you must be better or more loveable because you can do something relatively well. My ability to draw, or my progress in drawing well, didn't come because I struggled and fought the process; it came because it was a natural movement within myself.

The genuine artist doesn't create art because of a wanting to be an artist; the artist creates art because art is what moves within him/her. This cycle can repeat itself over and over and over again, until death, and the one seeking never realizes the delusion in their efforts. It can play out in the form of education as well; as when you see someone with a degree and therefore, have wonderful thoughts about him or her, such as, "Well if only I had a degree like them, then I would be happy and whole."

In relationships, you may see a couple that appears to be joyful and in your mind you contribute their joy as being caused by them being the perfect match, or being soul mates. This creates the chase that seeks a soul mate with the hope of finding Joy, not realizing that deeply joyful relationships have nothing to do with people completing each other, but rather it is when two people have learned to find joy independently of each other that creates such a magical space.

You'll even find the same cycle in the quest for financial gain. You may see someone who has money and project thoughts about how it's better than your life situation, as you believe their joy to be based upon their life circumstances. You then attribute well-being to money, creating the delusion that says it takes money to be happy and joyful; therefore if you do not have money, then by default you suffer.

All of this is taking place in your mind, this game of finding wholeness as if it's somewhere other than Here. This is how the vast majority of humankind spends their energy, which serves as a great lesson. If you pay attention, you quite clearly see that this movement in the mind to find wholeness externally is not only not working, but nor is it producing the results that you know deep down are waiting to be discovered.

> *The genuine artist doesn't create art because of a wanting to be an artist; the artist creates art because art is what moves within him/her.*

Returning to the skateboard example; here is how it might unfold from an Awakened State of living. Since I'm not searching for wholeness in the mind, I can watch the skateboarder do tricks without projecting a story that says his worth is better or worse than anyone else. I simply enjoy this experience for what it is, without attaching myself to it and becoming a slave to the mind.

Here is a defining point of this book. In an Awakened state, the only reason I would take on the task of learning the skateboarding tricks is because it appears to be a fun life experience to try. When you engage in life experiences with the intent of finding wholeness, you always set yourself up for internal dis-ease and life limitations. When you deeply discover your Wholeness as already Present and not deficient in any way, your life experience becomes focused on simply enjoying yourself, enjoying others, and enjoying Life.

You can see how taking on the task of skateboarding with the intent of enjoyment, creates less space for irritation, since if I'm not successful at completing a trick, my worth isn't defined by failure. When failure bothers you, it can only be a result of looking for self worth in that which you're chasing.

By living in a society that conditions you to believe that your worth is gained by accomplishment, this only perpetuates the illusion that self-worth is determined by achieving something. This is only created in the human mind, not in reality, and therefore, it doesn't create true sustenance, but only another dream in the mind... which is short lived.

> *When you engage in life experiences with the intent of finding wholeness, you always set yourself up for internal dis-ease and life limitations.*

Just as in becoming "famous," it's common for humans to think that the more people who like them will equal a more likable self; therefore, the chase ensues to become famous, popular, etc. In Truth though, your internal well being has nothing to do with other people liking or disliking you. The thoughts others have about you are not actually about you, they can only be thoughts about *their idea of you* based on their own projections; which is a dream version of you and not the Real you.

Living in Eternity, and not being a slave to mental concepts such as time, creates a space of genuine freedom where we are not bound by the quest to find worth and value. For within us, we have discovered an infinite amount of Love in this moment. We simply discover contentment, a peace, and a love that is sincerely without argument about what is, about whatever is showing in this moment.

Therefore, your movements as a human being are focused in this moment without an attachment to outcome; your activity in life becomes infinitely more enjoyable or peaceful as it is not determined so much by what you do but rather how you do it.

The beauty here is that from this space of freedom and contentment the mind calms down. It no longer becomes your master and returns to its proper place as servant. The mind runs when it's bound by time, but in Eternity, it finds a place of rest, as it discovers that there is really no place to go; everything is right now, in this eternal moment.

The thoughts others have about you are not actually about you, they can only be thoughts about their idea of you based on their own projections; which is a dream version of you and not the Real you.

Chapter 6
Love Clarification

Before getting much further into this, I feel it to be appropriate to bring clarity to this concept of Love. Quite sincerely, most people are confused about what Love *truly* is and how it relates to this teaching and the teachings of past sages and spiritual teachers. It's important that many of the misconceptions are dispelled so you can move forward with greater clarity.

To put it directly, Love is a dominant element which exists in Life's Natural state. Please understand, Life's Natural state is *beyond* what you think about Life's Natural state; it exists before the mind even thinks about it. To attempt to define it with words is a task that will never succeed; as all that can be done is to point towards it. What's most important is the direct experience of this Love, and from the experience of it you will know it more deeply.

Simply carrying ideas and beliefs *about* Love does nothing to *experience* it. Much like talking about water doesn't get you wet. No matter how much you think about water, or how much you believe water is wet, this does nothing when it comes to actually *experiencing* water. This actuality points to the silliness in *believing* in God. I suggest you directly experience the mystery of Life rather than merely thinking or holding onto ideas about Life's depth.

As I write about Love, please be clear that I'm pointing to something much deeper. By experiencing it from this depth, you are less likely to fall into the trap of believing in your thoughts *about* Love, and rather go straight for the actual experience of Love from within yourself.

I'm going to use the example of Father Daughter relationships to help clarify some points. As I play the role of father/step-father to three girls, these relationships have taught me a great deal about the depth of True Love.

What has been recognized deeply within my being is that no matter what my daughters do or don't do, I Love them all the same, wholly and completely. There is nothing they can do that makes me want to love them less, and another important point is that there is nothing they can do that makes me want to love them more. My Love for them is already infinite and without conditions.

It is true that not everyone has this experience with their children, and some look to their children's actions to define the level of Love they extend; but we'll get into how this creates only suffering later on.

The Love I have for my children is unconditional, which means there are no conditions which determine my

Love for them. What does it mean to extend Love in this manner? It could be expressed by not determining their value based on external events. Another way to look at this is to say I don't intend to withhold Love from them based on what they do or don't do.

As Love is undefinable by the mind, it is also undefinable in the sense of how it might unfold. How I express Love to my children may differ from how another might express this same Love, but nonetheless it is Love. It is a movement that doesn't argue with how life chooses to unfold; it is a movement that accepts fully, and in this, I don't argue with how life might unfold within my children. This isn't to say I have to agree with everything they do or don't do, it's merely to point to a Truth that knows who they are as not being defined by their actions, or even better, they are not defined by my *thoughts* about their actions.

An example... if my daughter happens to stub her toe on the sidewalk, I don't look at such an event and then believe that this event should not have happened, or that this event somehow means she's dumb or deficient in some way. I simply see it as a movement of life, and this is how life chose to unfold in that particular moment. She might learn from it, or she may not; but again, whether she learns or not is irrelevant as it pertains to the Love I extend to her.

It is quite common for parents to see such an event and to attach a story to it, a story that somehow desires to establish value, or to use the story as an excuse to withhold Love. The truth of the matter is that the stubbing of the toe was neither right nor wrong, good nor bad. Again, it doesn't mean we have to agree with the event or to pretend we enjoyed it, the point is to recognize that our judgments about the event are not true and not a valid justification for withholding Love.

This example of the stubbed toe can be universally transferred to any life event, however, the more your mental stories or judgments threaten your stories of personal identity, the more difficult it will be to see this truth clearly. For example, if I believe strongly that my daughter stubbed her toe due to my neglect in looking after her, I might use this story to determine my value as a parent. I could say it means that I'm not a good father for allowing such a thing to happen, and then chose to withhold love from myself through mental condemnation.

Because I attached her accident to my personal worth, in a sense it blinds me to the Truth that my value is *not* determined by such silliness. Again, if I am looking for my worth as a father or human being outside my Self, I enter into an asleep state and live from a dream in the mind.

When you have difficulty in seeing your most Divine Nature, it can only be caused by your clinging to something that is not True. Often, your clinging is done automatically as it is a product of conditioning. This is why you are encouraged to slow down, to live life with an Awareness that is focused on the moment at hand, rather than being so concerned with the content in your mind that wants to focus on something in the past or future.

The Love that I extend to my children is the same Love that Life is asking that I extend to the Whole of Existence. The good news is that Love is your natural state of Being, which in a sense is your True Identity. Such a thing might be difficult to understand now, which is fine; all I can suggest is... that you keep reading.

> *When you have difficulty in seeing your most Divine Nature, it can only be caused by your clinging to something that is not True.*

If Love is your natural state of Being, wherein lies the difficulty? Let me ask you a question, how much energy do you expend not being who you are, but trying to be who you think you should be? You have this absurd idea that who you are now is somehow unworthy, and you must do or become something other than what you are now in order to be acceptable or spiritually whole. Do you see this insanity playing out in your life?

How much energy do you expend arguing with what is, with reality, or arguing with your current life circumstances? When you are sad, do you want not to be sad? When you are angry, do you want not to be angry? Do you argue with what you do with your time? Do you argue about your past and potential future? Do you argue with the desires you have and say that they should not be there? You could ask such questions until you turn blue in the face.

If you are honest with yourself you could find quite a few things about reality that you argue with. Arguing with life is a form of opposing *what is*, a form of opposing reality as it is right now, and when you oppose Reality you do so with intent to reinforce your beliefs. You want to reinforce the beliefs so they can be used to define who you are. Like I said earlier, your attempt to hold onto beliefs is an attempt to find yourself, yet finding Self in the mind is an impossibility since what you are exists *before* the mind or deeper than the mind.

As this Love continues to unfold or explode within you, it manifests itself as an acceptance for all of Life. You notice how every life experience presents an opportunity to delve into a deeper Love; a deeper discovery of what you are. As a result you begin to see Life with new eyes; you see Life as being on your side rather than as an evil plot to keep you bound to limitation and fear. The experience of limitation and fear is a result of your resistance to how life is unfolding in this Eternal Moment.

Love is Life's natural state, and when you accept Life's natural state, Love becomes your experience. Initially this can be difficult to realize, and what really makes it difficult is the holding onto your judgments as you are unwilling to let go of your beliefs that want to argue with Reality. Did you ever notice that when you argue with Reality, you lose every time? Reality will remain as Reality, regardless of your thoughts about it, regardless of your arguments.

> *As this Love continues to unfold or explode within you, it manifests itself as an acceptance for all of Life.*

The most common misconception about Love is that it can be possessed or controlled, but truly this possessive love is not Love but rather an extension of a fear that is afraid of losing something. An example of this would be a love with conditions. I will love you, if..... This is really holding onto an argument that wants to control others, or life, as the self feels separate and unstable. Again, it's placing Love outside one's Self, saying that your well-being or internal stability is determined by external conditions.

Possessiveness is a delusion, which believes Love to be limited, and when you see it as limited you withhold it. Withholding Love doesn't create more Love; it puts Love in a box and restricts its flow. The only time you truly experience genuine Love is when you sincerely share Love. When you Love someone completely, you do so because you drop the arguments that say they are unlovable.

Just as when I play the role of father; I already accept my children as they are, and because I love them so deeply there isn't an argument in the whole universe that could convince me otherwise. Here is the gift though. Because I extend Love to my children, I experience this Love within my being.

Did you ever notice that when you are withholding Love, you are experiencing fear within you? If I put conditions on the Love I have for my children, when those conditions are threatened, meaning they do something that puts my Love for them in jeopardy, I withhold that Love until my conditions are restored. But... as I withhold Love, it is *I* who suffers; it is *I* who restricts Love's flow in my perceived world.

This is how the vast majority of human beings live out their existence as they go their whole life without realizing what True Love is, hanging on to the delusion that Love remains as an elusive mystery that rests outside of the self

As you withhold Love, you do so with the sole intent of protecting your identity, of protecting who you think you are. You do this because you want desperately to know yourself; you want to solidify your identity. The delusion, though, again, is that what's being protected is not who or what you truly are, but the thoughts and beliefs you use to define who you are, that which only exists as a dream in the mind.

> *As I withhold Love, it is I who suffers; it is I who restricts Love's flow in my perceived world.*

Here is a profound Truth that will surely disturb the beliefs of many people: If you can ever fall out of Love, then it was never Love you were in.

Most people are not in Love with others, but are searching for Love in hopeful expectations and prejudiced judgments, which means they are looking for Love in their thoughts *about* others, rather than in the *Reality* of others. If you look for Love in your thoughts, then you are seeing your thoughts to be more real than Reality.

Reality doesn't care about your thoughts, as it knows thought to be a tool used to function within Reality, rather than seeing Reality as a tool for your thoughts. This is why you see Reality as a threat, or something that opposes your existence. You have tied your identity to thought, and if you do so you will notice quite quickly that life isn't interested in serving your mental dream of a false self, but rather its interest is in serving Reality, which includes the Truth of what You are.

You see this idea of possessive love playing out in people's lives all the time. In relationships it manifests as a delusion that says, "I will only love you, if....." or, "If you do what I want you to do, I will love you, and if you do something that I don't want you to do, I will withhold love."

I encourage you to question such happenings in your own life. Where do you withhold love hoping it will protect who you are thought to be, and in this restriction of love has it ever led to a deeper unfolding of Love within your being?

If you are not ready to discover this deeper Love, then the Love I'm pointing to might sound rather dull and uneventful, but this is really a ploy to protect your false love, to protect the mental self you have attached to your possessive love. Often times it plays out in your mind as a fear that believes you won't be able to function with a Love that simply accepts life as it is. You wonder how the hell you can be who you are if you can't control who you love and whom you don't love?

Quite sincerely, if you have Love in your heart for some, while at the same time withholding Love from another, what you are experiencing is not Love per se, but rather you are experiencing an effort to reinforce who you *think* you are.

> *Reality doesn't care about your thoughts as it knows thought to be a tool used to function within Reality, rather than seeing Reality as a tool for your thoughts.*

Remember, Love isn't a movement that agrees or disagrees; it is a movement that simply doesn't argue with reality and fully embraces all that arises. People can disagree with each other and still Love, just as if my children would make a choice that I would not, it doesn't mean that they are now undeserving of my acceptance as a human being.

This, of course, creates a movement into a deeper acceptance beyond the superficial, beyond the exterior.

You find yourself accepting Self and others simply because you are here sharing this experience called life; and because Life accepts everyone without argument, you find yourself doing the same.

Arguments are a movement that opposes or proclaims something that **is** or should not be. If I make a decision that brings suffering, the suffering presents itself as an opportunity to grow and expand, and therefore suffering is valid as it serves my well-being by teaching me. Just as physical pain teaches me to pay more attention to what I'm doing, internal suffering teaches me to pay more attention to my perception of reality.

In this Truth, you can see how poor choices can actually be successes. Without the suffering, you would never Awaken to the colors of all things beautiful. Without physical pain, you might step on broken glass and never know that your foot was about to get infected, hindering your physical experience.

In my perception there are no bad choices, and no good choices, as all choices carry value and the choice you make in any given moment is the exact choice that needs to be made; it is completely acceptable regardless of any dreamed up judgments that float through your mind.

Please hear this, if you offer resistance to the choices you've made in the past, or the choices you will make in the future, you proclaim that what is should not be, and in a sense you run from it. When you run from the choices you've made, you confess that they are without value and blind yourself from the lessons waiting to unfold.

Regret and guilt also keep you from Awakening to a more Realized Self, which is another form of condemning Reality that only restricts Love's flow. As you accept your choices and the choices of others with more sincerity, it's as if a flood gate has opened up and you gain valuable insight into how you might experience this Explosion of Love with greater depth and clarity.

Can you see how a life spent in opposition or in resistance keeps you bound to limitation and fear? Let's say for example someone feels led to pick up this book, but as they read something in the beginning that seems to threaten their current belief structure, they lay the book down and miss something that might be trying to reach a deeper part of them. This certainly isn't to say one must read this; it is simply to point out how we limit ourselves by clinging to the content in the mind.

> *When you run from the choices you've made, you confess that they are without value and blind yourself from the lessons waiting to unfold.*

Chapter 7
Who Am I

Who Am I? It's an age old question that most, if not all, have asked at some point in their lives. It's the question encouraged by a Heart that desires to know what's True. Who is this One who sits now, in this moment experiencing Life from behind these eyes? What is this Presence of myself?

This question is also the doorway to enter into a profoundly deep life experience. I'm going to ask you to approach this question with a courageous sincerity, in a way that most have never approached such a question before. First, recognize your depth by realizing deeply that Life is *beyond* your thoughts. Life is something that cannot be defined with words.

Instead of asking, *Who Am I?* Let us sincerely ask, *What Am I Not?*

Is it true that you are "good?" This question points to the relative nature of all labels and concepts, which I want to clarify here. I'm not asking if you *think*, *believe*, or *hope*. I'm asking if it's really, really True. It might help you to place yourself back out into the universe in your meditative spot and sincerely ask this question.

After a while of meditating on this question, you might have the insightful follow up question of, "Good compared to what?" In a relative sense, everyone can potentially be "good," for example, at playing the piano, if you compare yourself to someone with no arms. The one who has no arms can compare their piano playing ability to that of a cockroach.

For you to be good you must make a judgment or comparison with someone else you think is *not* good. In your own Presence or in the Awareness of what you *Truly* are, as you meditate in this space that has nothing to compare itself to, ask yourself, "Is it true that I am *good*?" Remember, for you to be *good*, you must create a thought that says *bad*. Again, I'm not asking your opinion, I'm asking that you go deeply into the Reality that is Here and Now. If you look to the mind to make comparisons, it's not looking into Now, but into the past or future as it searches for some event to make comparisons to.

Say for example you ask the question, "Am I good?" You may look at an experience of when you were twelve and compare yourself to a childhood friend who you believed was better at being good than you were. Where is this activity or movement to discover Truth taking place? Is it in Reality or is it in the dream of your mind? Does it Truly exist Now, in this moment, or are you creating some fanciful story using the imagination in the mind?

You are discovering the Truth of YOU and not the truth in the mind. If you look for Truth in the mind, you will never discover Truth. Everything that passes through the mind is not real and is only an interpretation that stems from your conditioning. It is an attempt to define the undefinable.

See clearly that you're not really "*good*," and this idea of *good* is not Truth but a movement in the mind that makes dualistic and relative comparisons. If you can see this, I'm very sincere when I say that within you in this moment is the Awareness necessary to Awaken to the fullness of you. You are but a tiny shift away from seeing the colors of all things Beautiful. Cheers.

If this still is unclear, I simply encourage you to spend uninterrupted quiet time investigating this movement in the mind that wants to see *good* as Real. In addition to this, keep reading.

As this concept of *good* falls away as something that is not true and returns to its place as something that happens in the mind, you can see how its opposite, *bad*, is not true either. So now ask yourself with sincerity, "Is it true that I am bad?"

I'm not referring to good and bad as a point of preference, such as that it might be true that you think something such as lawn mulch tastes bad. I'm referring to the Truth of Reality. Just because you proclaim that lawn mulch tastes bad, is it *true* that lawn mulch is bad, or tastes bad for everyone and everything?

Good and bad are two extensions of the same thing. They are simply two opposite extremes of perception, but do not define something. As this insight sinks deeper and deeper into your awareness, you may be able to see how to give up the mental fight of trying to define something as good or bad, which is the creation of judgment. The mental fight is seen as a battle that can never really be won as it is a battle that doesn't even exist in Reality. In trying to define yourself as good, there will always be the potential to find something to compare yourself to, which makes you seem bad from the mind's perspective.

Round and round goes the mental movement that searches for Self but never pins it down, nor finds the Self that *is* True. The mind wants to hang onto labels and concepts such as good and bad, hoping they can tell us who we are. Much of this is just silly conditioning that you've picked up from a society that innocently operates from a very limited and fear based world view or perception which is sprung only from ignorance.

Most human beings believe that when they place a label on something, they define it. Again, another example is by calling our land by specific names and then defending those names as if they were real. You may call other people bad, and then treat them as such to reinforce that those beliefs are true.

If my daughters tell me I'm the best dad ever and someone challenges this statement resulting in me getting bothered internally, then it's a clear indication that I am looking for my identity in the thoughts of other people, or in the opinions of my daughter. This isn't to say that I discourage my daughters from expressing such a movement within them if that's what wants to arise, but it simply means that I don't attach myself to their comments.

The concept of duality implies that there exists two. This means that if there is good, there must also be bad, or if there is heads then there must also be tails. Duality is a swinging of sorts, from one side to another on a relative scale. This is much like the experience of hot and cold as you can only have "hot" if you compare it to "cold." One can't exist without the other.

Sometimes I find humor when my daughter says that the water is too hot, yet if I were to take a shower in the same temperature, I would call it too cold as I enjoy very hot showers. So who's right, my daughter or I, pertains to our observation about the water's temperature?

You cannot define any truth in dualistic observations, because Truth is non-dualistic and does not rest in the mind. It is only the mind that creates duality. The actual separation that we create between the experience of hot and cold does not actually exist. If you ask if the water is hot or cold, from a Truth standpoint, all you can say is that the water simply is as it is, neither hot nor cold, not good nor bad. It just is what it is.

And since it is what it is, life fully accepts it as completely valid. How can you be sure that Life accepts it? Simply because it is here and Life allows it to be. In each moment, everything that presents itself is fully accepted by Life, for Life knows that everything that arises serves a higher purpose that helps life to continue on in its infinite ways.

When this insight about duality penetrates your being, you may get the urge to begin eliminating duality from your perception. You take on a misguided identity that wants to align with Truth, and then avoid labeling things such as hot and cold, good and bad. It's as if you take on a new spiritual persona that wants to force the Awakening process.

Let me be clear, this is not *true* Awakening. To go around and pretend to see clearly by adopting spiritual talk and language is only to delude yourself further. How silly to converse with others and point out how their speech isn't true or relevant. We'll talk more later about how

Awakening might unfold and what the traps are that keep us in an asleep state.

Let's regroup and get back to Who Am I? You might be able to see more clearly that as you ask the question, "Who Am I Not?" you can see that you sincerely are not good, and are not bad. For such a thing is a dualistic observation that doesn't point to Truth but merely points to mental movements and conditioning.

The point here is to look at how much energy you invest in your mind that pertains to an attempt to solidify your worth as good or bad, or to judge others as good or bad. In addition to that, let's point out that the labels of right and wrong fall into this same realm of duality. Therefore, trying to determine which decisions are right and wrong in an Absolute sense is a game that goes nowhere.

Initially, the mental recognition of this insight might only offer a small degree of relief, as you are still conditioned with thought processes that have made its life mission to determine that which can never be determined. Be of good cheer though, because the point is not to merely understand such wisdom mentally, but rather to let this wisdom penetrate your heart, which in its own time will allow the insight to transform your perception.

We can also look at other delusions wrapped in duality that you use to define yourself and only create suffering. One example is the label of smart and dumb. You can only be smart if you accept that someone else is stupid. Granted that, yes, others may make decisions that appear dumb, but in Truth those decisions are their perfect life learning opportunity. To label it as dumb and to believe your label to be true is a form of proclaiming others' decisions have no value; which is to again resist Life's flow, restricting the Love that desires to explode from within you.

> *The point here is to look at how much energy you invest in your mind that pertains to an attempt to solidify your worth as good or bad or to judge others as good or bad.*

For those who desperately want to cling to the idea of being smart, will spend much time and mental energy pointing out those they believe are dumb; for smart cannot exist without the label of dumb. Notice how the movement of the mind that wants to engage in such activity is not focused on now but focused on the dream in the mind.

As you become willing to see what is True, you give up the quest to use labels that you now know holds no Truth whatsoever; as you become more willing, your attention becomes more focused on where Truth *actually* resides, which is in this moment alone. For Reality exists only in now, and the more your attention is focused on now, the more Life can show you who and what you Truly are.

To sit in silence and question what you are, or what you are not is a practice known as Self-Inquiry. As you gain clarity into the Truth of Self, you automatically gain clarity about the whole of existence. It is this movement of discovery that will serve as your lifeline in waking up. However, most human beings will not engage in this practice and I'll tell you why.

As with the example of smart and dumb, people attach themselves to these labels and desperately believe them to be true. So to enter into a space that might suggest that the dream is not true is the equivalent to dying inside. You can see this play out with great enthusiasm regarding the label of "Christian."

If you have created an identity around the label of being a Christian, then to enter into the unknown and learn that this label means nothing other than the meaning you give it; you will find yourself with anxiety and fear about the possibility of discovering it's not really true.

I want to note that I'm not beating up on Christians but only use these references because of my own previous experience with clinging to this label; so it only makes sense that I would reference it. Regardless though, surely there will be those who think this book is a threat to the Christian ideology. Silly humans.

Is it True that the label of "Christian," can define your depth? Please substitute this label for any other label that you've noticed has been used to find identity. To a southern Baptist, the meaning of being a Christian can be quite different from that of a Pentecostal Christian. Who's right? By now you know it's irrelevant and yet it won't take long to find an argument of two people debating which one is the right one.

Even more absurd is the argument that it can be defined for all people. Some denominations will proclaim theirs is the *only* path, while others say you'll go to hell if you accept this or that denomination. Sure, these can be seen as extremes, and they are all extremes if you believe them to be true; as none of them are Ultimately True.

This, of course, is the perfect learning though. By no means am I saying this kind of activity should not go on; for all human beings are free to perceive how they choose. The suggestion I make is to look closely at your perceptions to see if your belief in them creates suffering in your life.

To investigate these labels in silence, you must first be willing to accept that you may not be who you are thought to be, and at first this takes courage. If you sincerely believe that you are your labels, and then your labels die, it can feel as though you die. To know that what you have believed all of your life never was true, can be a very real experience of heartache. It is a new birth.

> *For Reality exists only in now, and the more your attention is focused on now, the more Life can show you who and what you Truly are.*

If you go into this Self-Inquiry with a hidden agenda to support your mental dream, then you may only experience frustration or a deepening of delusion. You must really be willing to let it all go and begin again to see life with new eyes. Often, Awakening occurs after tremendous hardship, once it is fully realized that you don't know anything and become sincerely humbled.

It's not to say hardship is a required prerequisite to Awakening, it is just that hardship and suffering often soften the heart and make space for new insight. In Truth, all it really takes is sincerity. Sincerity is simply being honest with yourself. To put it more directly; it is honesty to admit that you don't know... that you don't know what to do, that you don't know who you are, and nor do you know the future.

However, we live in a society that believes sincerity to be a weakness. So people spend their whole lives trying to convince themselves that they *do* know what to do, they *do* know who they are, and they know how Life will or should unfold.

We call this worldly confidence, yet in silence the most worldly confident people suffer. The suffering manifests itself as a fear of losing what they are most confident about. This fear takes the shape of anger, treating others poorly, not being genuinely honest, hidden sadness and the like.

Such a movement of worldly confidence is rewarded by society because it is thought to be the answer to the inadequacy we feel. You think that if you could have certainty about your actions, about who you are, and about the future, you could then relax and have peace. This is a delusion that has infested the collective consciousness of mankind.

Please see clearly here, I am not suggesting this sort of confidence is wrong or should not be, nor am I saying that it has less value than a different kind of confidence. The mind is so quick to assume that because I'm talking about it, I must be trying to define it as right or wrong which is simply not the case. The invitation is simply to look at your own experience and discern if your interpretation of this writing can point to your source of suffering.

If there is a key, it is sincerity. Who hasn't had the experience of being honest, even though it hurt, only to find freedom waiting for you with open arms? A good cry is often a friend of sincerity. Hanging onto false confidence hurts, but you keep pushing forward because your conditioning tells you that false confidence is the way to liberation, but in Truth it only leads you down a path that has no end. It is like believing if you just got that promotion, your suffering would subside.

The challenge here is that your moments of sincerity are often short lived as you continue to engage in the game of pretending that everything is fine when you really know your heart is broken. You may pretend that you are *not* sad when sadness is happening. You may pretend that you are *not* angry, when anger is happening. You may pretend to know what to do, when in Truth you have no clue.

Awakening happens when you lay it all down and fully admit that Life is undefinable in the mind. For when you try to define life by holding onto your labels or trying to get life to conform to your mental dream, it is at that moment you become lost.

What am I, if I am not these labels?

At this point, I'm tempted to just stop. Going any further into this question can be a two-edged sword. As you empty your mind of all the labels, judgments, and ideas that you've used to define yourself with, it can be very easy from this point to just find new labels. It's easy because with new labels it can almost seem as a new beginning, and with this comes a sense of relief that is sprung from the release of old labels.

Such a thing can have value, however, it is not my intent to give you something else to cling to in the replacement of some other delusion. If you did such a thing, it would be similar to that of one who bounces around from one religion to another, or from one belief to another, believing something new has been found, and constructing a new self-center around new ideas.

Do you see though how this practice of bouncing around only substitutes one delusion for another, rather than helping you to fully wake up? Don't get me wrong, such a thing can lead you to a willingness to just let it all go, however, I'm going straight for the heart of the matter, with no detours.

> *When you try to define life by holding onto your labels or trying to get life to conform to your mental dream, it is at that moment you become lost.*

What am I, if I am not these labels?

Imagine yourself in silence. You are all alone with your present awareness, your simple but profound existence. As you watch yourself breathe, just notice the breath. I'm not asking for the mind to comment on it, I'm simply inviting you to be aware of this moment. Do you notice the presence of you? Again, not the mental comments about you, but just the awake-ness, or the awareness of you, the same Presence that has been there your whole life, the part of you that has been unchanged.

This is the real you, behind the facade. This is the One behind the sound, behind the breath, the One who all this is happening to. This is the honest you. This is the you that exist before everything outside you.

If you find difficulty in feeling this Presence that I'm pointing to, it is because you are trying to find it with comments from your mind. Give the mind permission to rest, even if only just for this moment so that you may hear the sound of your soul.

Can you sense the most primary element of your humanness? The part of you that just simply is *here,* is always *here*, and is always in this moment? What is this that rests?

Yes, it is true that such a thing can be difficult to notice if the mind is so chaotic. The mind has become a distraction, a point of interest that now serves as an addiction. However, it isn't so much the mind itself as it is our addiction to its content. The mind does what it does, but when you look at its movement with focused attention, you empower its Presence. Most people energize the content of the mind so intensely that it seems to overtake them.

If you are caught up in this movement, your focus is not on the Reality of what you are, but rather it is chained to the mind's content, as you have become a slave to your addiction.

If you find this invitation to be difficult, to sense your most primary Self, I invite you to become open to establishing some sort of devotion that gives regular attention to the healing of this addiction. As you do so, you discover tiny gaps in your thoughts. In the quiet space between thoughts, healing waits to be discovered. I'll spend more time later on addressing this point of devotion as a practice for calming the energy of your mind.

As you begin to see this Presence within you that has always been there with more clarity, I ask with great sincerity: What is This?

In asking the question, What is This? You are invited to ask without seeking an answer, rather than asking as if it's an acknowledgment from within yourself that says you are willing to discover something other than what you *think* you know. Your most profound Spiritual insights will come from asking deep questions without looking for an answer.

See the depth in this. When you ask a question, usually the mind has some sort of outcome in mind or an agenda. There is often times an answer that is hoped for, and because of this you may find yourself asking manipulative questions to get the answers you want to hear. This isn't genuine Self- Inquiry.

Asking with genuine Conscious intent is a movement of sincerity, deep honesty, and deep discovery. If you want to know the deepest Truths, you must let go of **everything** that is thought to be true. For if you enter into Self-Inquiry believing that you know something, you reject anything that might threaten what you *think* you already know, which, of course, restricts the flow of Truth.

This points towards a most sincere willingness, humility, and courage beyond measure. I say this because the One who wishes to discover the most amazing depth of

Self, must be *willing* to give up everything that is clung to in the mind. To enter into this space, you must be totally naked.

You must give up the idea that says you are better than anyone else. You must give up the notion that others are less loveable. You must let go of the belief that says you know what is right and wrong; good and bad, as it relates to what happens in your world.

The question is… do you know with certainty that others are less loveable or do you only think that? Do you know with great certainty that what other people do is wrong or do you just believe that? To proclaim that you *know* it as Truth, as absolute, you are saying that your "right" is the only "right," your "good" is the only "good." Or this may be more appropriately stated, as… your God is the only God.

What do you know with absolute certainty? For the serious student I would suggest you stop right now and go sit quietly for thirty minutes and let such a question penetrate your core, before continuing. This is not a trick question. There is a very real and profound discovery waiting to be seen, and it rests in the One thing which you *can* know with absolute certainty.

The difference between *knowing* something and *believing* something is that in *knowing* something zero doubt exists. To say you are ninety-nine percent sure is also to say that you don't *know*, you only *believe*. This is something that I don't need to spend much time on, since if you simply get honest with yourself, you will recognize that much of what you *think* you know is *not* what you know but only what you *believe*.

To believe in something is not to **know** it but only to see it as possible. For when you **know**, belief is no longer necessary. In a sense it's kind of like believing there is a hand at the end of your arm when you're staring right at it. It's not necessary to believe that which is clear as day.

This is the clarity I point to; *knowing* with certainty what is True about the Truth of You. Perhaps it would be more appropriately stated as a clarity that points towards a knowing of what you are *not*.

As this Truth becomes more and more clear, suffering falls away and conflict drops. This is simply because suffering is a result of not seeing the Self clearly, and looking to find the Self externally where Self is not.

By realizing the Self cannot be good or bad, you give up the fight that wants to define Self, Others, and Life as good or bad. Of course, it is not to say that this fight ends completely right away, for you must allow this Truth to penetrate deep within your being. You must *embody* the Truth, rather than merely *think* about it.

This embodiment occurs naturally as you become more and more willing to lay down the fight as it arises. If you get into an argument about who is right and who is wrong, this Truth releases the need to expend energy on something that can never be defined. Thus leaving you available to not engage in an experience that creates suffering or conflict, allowing you to remain as you are, rather than giving chase after a self that can only be whole if an argument is perceived as being won.

This is the unfolding of Light in your world; to see Truth, and allow fear to fall away. This is the meaning behind the words; Truth shall set you Free.

> *Your most profound Spiritual insights will come from asking deep questions without looking for an answer.*

Chapter 8
Light & Darkness

Light is the Truth of Reality. Darkness is the absence of this Light, of Truth. When you live from anywhere other than Truth, it is as if your world becomes dark. When I say dark, I mean in the sense of living asleep. In this darkness, you become confused and unguided, as you simply cannot see clearly. In darkness, you serve the dream that blinds you to the Light of Truth, of Reality.

This pointer toward Light and dark has been referenced for thousands of years. It has taken the form of stories that use concepts and imagery with the hope of pointing to the Truth within you. However, you have perverted this pointer with the intent of defining one as right and one as wrong. In saying that darkness is wrong, you proclaim it is void of value and therefore, run from it.

In your running from darkness, you miss the lesson that simply wants to point to Light. You run as if the solution is somewhere *out there*, so you run to the external, hoping it will take away the darkness. The Truth of the matter is that there is nothing external or outside you that can remove the darkness, nor is there anything outside you that can create the Light you crave so desperately.

Turning on the Light is simply a matter of openness and perception. Just like when you argue about something that means nothing, the moment you see clearly the irrelevance of your argument, you give up the argument. In giving up the argument or in seeing clearly, you return to your Natural state; the state where conflict does not reside.

All of your suffering is simply an indication that there is an absence of Light, an absence of seeing Reality clearly. What keeps you in the dark is your insistence upon holding on to non-truth with an attempt to solidify who you *think* you are. You hold on to the self that wants to be right, you hold on to the self who wants to know who is wrong. Again, such things are unknowable since such things do not even Truly exist in Reality.

> *In saying that darkness is wrong, you proclaim it is void of value and therefore run from it.*

The movement of Light transcends good and bad, for it sees both as equally valid. Light represents clarity, it represents Life's most Natural state of Being and when you see life as it naturally is, this Light enters your world and transforms everything.

To illustrate how this plays out in your world, can you imagine coming across a most beautiful rose? With this rose, comes a vine that is full of thorns. As you attempt to grab the vine, you notice the pain that comes with being stuck by the thorns. If your perception is clouded, you might notice that the vine is coming out of the dirt and you begin to stomp on the dirt as if it was responsible for your pain. You may kick, scream, and blame as you become convinced that the source of your pain stems from the dirt.

Just as in your personal suffering, you tend to kick and scream by blaming others and life events as the culprit. Clarity happens when you pay more attention to the moment and realize that what hurts is holding on. As it becomes more and more clear that the suffering is created by your insistent effort to hold on to that which was never meant to be held on to, what happens?

Quite simply and naturally you let go. The result of letting go is the end of suffering in that Eternal moment.

When you are clear, notice how there is no effort on your part to let go. Seeing that your pain is a result of hanging on, you realize that you can still enjoy the flower and share its space. However, there isn't a need to hold on to it, or possess it.

This is why striving to Awaken is pointless. By turning Awakening into a goal, it insinuates that there is a necessary effort on your part. In Truth, all it takes is a willingness to see clearly. The natural state of your hand is to be open; just as the natural state of your Being is to be open as well.

The effort comes from *believing* you must do something in order to experience wholeness, which is a delusion that keeps you from seeing clearly. For if you believe you must do something, you constantly look to the future to find wholeness, rather than recognizing it as already Present. Such a thing can keep you blinded for many years, or many lifetimes.

Just as in holding water, if you grasp at it, it slips through your fingers. If you hold open your hands and gently allow it to be, it stays with you. This points to an effortless way of living that awaits you as you become the One who sees Life clearly. It may seem as if it takes tremendous effort to live life, this is only because you feel separate from Life, thinking you must do something in order to be fulfilled.

What is being missed is that you are not separate from Life's movement. The same force that moves the planet around the sun is the same power that wants to move through you. However, you have created a limited self that believes its power to be very limited, and because this is believed as true, it becomes your experience; just as you believe a stick to be a rattlesnake, you become fearful.

It can seem to be a scary thing to just let go and allow Life to do what it does. However, this fear of letting go is an attempt to protect something that isn't even there; so the more you allow clarity to arise, you discover with great ease that letting go is very natural. In this, you may see that what is being asked of you is not necessarily to let go but only to see clearly. As you see clearly, this letting go happens naturally.

Allow a sense of Freedom to be recognized as you realize that you don't have to find the effort to let go, but only to have the willingness to see what is True and then letting go will happen in its perfect timing. In this way you won't feel as though you are incomplete or invalid, if you don't let go, or if you don't do something.

Your wholeness isn't determined by action, or even by seeing because you already *are* whole. Although to experience your wholeness as Reality, you must see the Self clearly. So seek not to find wholeness, but rather be willing to see the barriers that obstruct your vision from seeing your True and Whole Self, as you are in this moment.

This is similar to saying that you are already Enlightened, and you only un-enlighten your experience by hanging on to that which is not real. You separate yourself from Now, by looking for yourself where you are not. You can see how this unfolding isn't necessarily a game of finding yourself, but rather a game of discovering the roadblocks that keep you from seeing the Self you have always been.

> *Seek not to find wholeness, but rather be willing to see the barriers that obstruct your vision from seeing your True and Whole Self, as you are in this moment.*

This Truth can create a dramatic change of focus, turning your quest inward rather than looking for a self that exists externally. If you insist on finding yourself, you are proclaiming that you are not here already. Therefore, the simple act of looking for a self implies that you are not the Self. This simple act, or movement of perception creates an experience where you feel separate from Life, as you convince yourself that your wholeness must be found in some other moment than now.

The power of insight is that it acts like a wind in your sail to help you to realign perception to be more in alignment with your highest Self. The challenge, though, is to recognize the wind or the insight, not as the Light itself, but rather as just a pointer to the Light that you already are.

You can see this play out as you cling to words, believing that the words must be right because they assist in your growth or discovery. However, the Light is not in the words, the Light is in the One who is open to see the Truth within oneself. If you are fooled into believing that the words are where the discovery comes from, you put the Light outside the Self once again.

I will use my own experience as an illustration. During the years I spent as a devout Christian, there was the innocent belief that Christianity must be the right answer because it helped me to let go in some areas, which allowed for a deeper joy; therefore, I protected the dogmas as if they held my liberation. In doing this, I exchanged one form of clinging for another, instead of letting go of *all* clinging.

This is simply part of the process, so no need to beat yourself up for not seeing it clearly the first time around. I say this because in a sense it all adds up. Your life experiences lead you towards the Light, regardless of your judgments about your experiences. It's not to say that being a Christian, or adopting Christian beliefs are wrong. The question is are you limiting your discovery by believing that your Light is in something external?

You can see that being a Christian is a chosen path rather than a solution, since the real solution is what you already are. In this Truth, there is the Freedom that comes with not having to protect your beliefs by condemning those who do not follow your chosen path. Because you now know that Truth or Light is in the Being and not in a belief, you can give others the freedom to discover it as they see fit.

The only reason you would have difficulty in accepting the path of another is because internally you are unsure about your own path. You may believe that if you can convince others to choose your path or to deny their own, your path must be the right path. So you expend tremendous amounts of energy attempting to convince others that they are not whole unless they believe what you believe. Or even better, you expend energy on simply not accepting the path that others choose.

The Truth of the matter is that wholeness is already what you are; therefore, any path that is seen as something that can make you more whole, more acceptable or more lovable, is a path that leads you away from what you already are. The purpose of a path is to help you see more clearly what you already are, so the question becomes... is it truly helping?

Just because a path might have seemed helpful in the past, doesn't automatically mean it is helpful for you today. Baby food can help a child to thrive, but it doesn't mean it always will. Sooner or later you will have to let go of old nourishment, and discover a deeper nourishment if you wish to expand your experience into deeper depths of Love and Light.

It is like holding on to the idea that the world is flat without remaining open to the possibility that it can be of some other shape too. It doesn't mean you have to swallow the idea that it might be round, but you don't shut yourself off to the possibility that it might be.

There is a state of openness here that allows you to remain unattached to anything, and open to everything. In this openness, the voice that wants to guide you becomes louder. Initially, there is a fear that is afraid to be that open, as the belief says that if you do not believe or attach yourself to something, you'll somehow be left wide open to become a victim.

You might be able to see here how such a thought or fear believes that your well-being is determined by what happens in the mind. So obviously, if this is your stance, you cling to your beliefs, or your fears, as you sincerely believe that they protect you. When you believe they protect you, you hold onto them with great force.

Your belief tries to protect itself and does so because you believe your beliefs to be true or real. You perceive your beliefs to be what you are, and therefore, the thought of your belief not being true, insinuates that *you* are not real, that you are not true.

Closing yourself off to the possibility that what you believe might be limiting your experience is the equivalent of sitting in darkness and ignoring the possibility that your world could perhaps become brighter by simply switching on a light. As you open yourself up to admit that you don't really know, Life comes rushing in with a wind that will move you into a clearer perception.

Chapter 9
The Game of Ego

Ego can be defined many different ways, so I want to bring clarity to how I use this word. "Ego" makes reference to the imaginary identity we hold in the mind. I am not saying that we have one ego or one mental creation of who we think we are; ego encompasses all ideas about our self that exist in the mind.

For example, to say that I am a writer is to make reference to an ego, simply because what I am cannot be defined as a writer, but rather writing is merely something that happens on occasions within my experience. The Ego is that idea of self that perceivable exists separately from all that you see 'out there.'

To bring clarity to one of the most common misconceptions about ego, I want to point to a Truth that doesn't see ego as a threat or as something that should not be, but rather it accepts it fully as having an equal right to be. Ego, like everything else, can be a fantastic teacher, and therefore, seeing it as something to get rid of is only another means of resisting Life.

As you give up this fight that wants to rid itself of ego, you might see more clearly that the only thing that wants to get rid of ego is another ego. The only reason you would want to rid yourself of ego is because you believe that without ego you would be more whole. Again, this is to place your wholeness in an imaginary tomorrow.

We all carry ideas about who we are thought to be, including the most Enlightened Beings. It is a natural movement of the mind to create a mental self to help one function within this Reality. What makes the difference is to question if you are being fooled into believing that the ego is Real. If you believe the ego is who you are, you move on its behalf as its servant.

As life is lived to serve the ego, you end up serving your thoughts, rather than the Reality that is True, Here and Now. If you serve thought as if it is real, and when thought is threatened to be proven unreal you go into reactive mode and respond with fear, which only deepens the limitations you experience in Life.

In your mind you have a self that has been created and if you take time to be silent, this can be seen clearly. All you must do is question who you *think* you are. This also points back to self-inquiry and asking what you are not. Ego is what you are *not*. Initially when you ask the question, "Who am I?" Your mind races to produce answers based on your experience. You may get answers such as a father, a mother, a son, or daughter.

> *The Ego, is that idea of self that perceivable exists separately from all that you see 'out there.'*

Another example of this *'thought* of Self' is the ego based good self or bad self, right self or wrong self. In Truth though, as we've learned, such labels are not True, but rather comparisons and judgments that only exist in the mind and not in Reality.

You can see the difficulty that is created by clinging to this ego, which manifests as suffering. If you believe your True Self to be "bad," you experience the suffering that comes with attaching to such a thought. If you believe your True Self to be "good," with this comes the suffering of trying to prove others as bad; this may manifest as non-acceptance for others just so we can feel good by maintaining this false belief.

There is a serious and profound wisdom in seeing clearly that you are **not** the ego, and as you see this more clearly, you give up the fight that wants to serve the ego. In your letting go of this fight, you naturally move into an alignment with your True Self which is not bound by fear and limitation. I'll explain why:

Your experience as a human being is predominantly determined by your perception, as you create your world through how you see the world. If you see yourself as an ego, what you see is a self that is separate from life, a self which is limited to an imaginary label that is afraid of losing who it is you are *thought* to be.

This isn't to say that you should then start seeing yourself as some other label in the mind, but rather is to say that you give up seeing your True Self with the mind, period. It is to say that you stop looking at the mind to tell you who you are. In doing so, you create space for the True Self to make itself known. It would be an easy assumption in the mind to say that because I'm not this, then I must be that. This simply isn't true.

To do such a thing is to continue the delusion that what you are is some sort of mental creation, a dualistic something. I recommend that you *feel* what you are, rather than trying to *think* about what you are. Yes, it is true that you will never be able to clearly define what you are through the tool of the mind.

> *Your experience as a human being is predominantly determined by your perception, as you create your world through how you see the world.*

The original intent of the mind was never meant to find yourself, but rather its function is to help you live out your existence, it is a tool. The mind's ability is beyond what we comprehend today; its creative power far exceeds the limitations we've placed on it. The challenge, though, is that we are using the mind in a way that creates limited life experiences rather than an abundant life experience.

Everything that has been created in this world by human beings passed first through the mind as a seed, from this place it manifests into the physical world. You can see from here how it makes sense if you see yourself as a separate human being who has to struggle to survive, the universe offers back what you project.

The universe doesn't discriminate against the thoughts you project; you simply get back what you give. If you see your world to be problematic and limited, the universe will show you that such a thing can be created and experienced. You are this powerful.

At this point, it is very common to now try and figure out how you can change your thoughts in order to create a life experience that will fulfill all your desires. The delusion, though, is you still have the belief that getting what you want will make you happy or whole. So I will throw out a heavy caution: the one who is determined to find wholeness through the fulfillment of desire will be on a never-ending quest.

I only share such insight with you about how Life gives back what you project, not so you can learn how to manipulate reality, but only so you might wake up to the complete goodness that is already you.

If you'd like, feel free to take such insight and use it to try and get what you want, but if you'd like to go deeper, hold off a bit on constructing a plan to take over the world, and stick with this discovery of Awakening.

It's worthwhile to point out that the one who desperately wants something that is beyond this moment is the *ego* searching for wholeness. Let's look at it more closely. Say, there is a house that you desperately want to call your own, and you're willing to do anything to get it. You even experience some anxiety as you think about acquiring this house and becoming its owner. Within you,

If you see your world to be problematic and limited, the universe will show you that such a thing can be created and experienced.

there is a feeling that if you have this, it would somehow make your life more meaningful or complete. Is this True?

To believe that something outside you can make you more whole or complete is to project that you are not whole in this moment, and therefore, your experience becomes what you project. Is it True that you are un-whole in this moment? It is one thing to say no I am not, but if you find yourself with anxiety or unbalanced excitement, it's a clear sign that what you are seeking is perceived to hold your well-being.

Yes, I know I'm repeating myself.

Sincerity plays a huge role here, because you cannot deceive Life, you can only be dishonest with yourself. It doesn't matter if you tell me that you're not seeking wholeness in that which you want, for Life will give you what you project.

If you get honest with yourself, all you need to ask is... What am I truly searching for? Am I looking for something to make me feel accepted, liked, loved or make me feel whole in any way?

Initially, you might think this means if you notice you're seeking wholeness, you shouldn't move forward; this isn't the case. Remember, this isn't so much about what you do or don't do; it's about how you perceive. So in realizing that you are seeking a delusion, if you feel led to do so then continue on, just this time continue on with a deeper awareness.

As you move, watch your movement, pay attention to the anxiety or any other emotion that may arise. This isn't about some monumental battle that requires you to struggle or change yourself through personal will; it is about seeing reality clearly. The deeper the clarity, the deeper the transformation.

It might seem too simplistic to only use your Awareness and not personal will, but this again is just the mind projecting that it must be a struggle. The ego loves using personal will, for it seems to validate the separate self. Question this thought: is it true that you must struggle in order to see clearly and allow for change to happen?

A good example of this might be when you realize, after years of holding on, that a person whom you thought wronged you, never really did. Upon this realization of what is *actually* true, you don't have to struggle to let go of the blame that hurts your being, you simply drop it with great ease. This is the beauty of Truth, when it is seen clearly the darkness falls away naturally.

Sometimes, it won't drop away as soon as you would like, and this is okay; just give Truth the freedom to flow through you. To rush it, or to believe that the process should happen faster, is just another form of resistance, which only restricts the flow even further. The only thing that wants to rush it is an ego that believes it will be more whole when it happens, which again projects wholeness to some other time than now.

The power of your Being lies in how you perceive. If you perceive Life from the standpoint of an ego, or as a indefinable label that is separate from the whole of Life, your experience will reflect that of a human being who is separate from God or separate from their True Self. Do you see your mentally created self as a Reality or as just a dream in the mind?

How can Life support you if you run around the earth believing you are separate from Life? How can you discover the wholeness in this moment if you run around believing your wholeness is somewhere other than here, right now? How can you be what you are when you are so concerned with being or becoming a self that lives only in your mind?

For this Explosion of Love to unfold within you, you must be willing to discover a Love that is *already* here. To see the colors of all things beautiful, you must stop chasing a beauty that is thought to only exist in tomorrow. You can see how chasing this Awakening or chasing wholeness does nothing but keep you at a perceived distance from it. The distance that is experienced is only perceived, though it's not Real.

In Truth, there is no distance between you and your highest Self, for how can someone be distant from what they actually are? Much like how you can compare your spiritual journey with that of another, you can look at someone and say... "Geez, I've got a long way to go." It only seems long because you compare yourself to another, and then you put requirements on your Awakening, saying you can't be Awake until you are more like this person.

> *If you perceive Life from the standpoint of an ego, or as a indefinable label that is separate from the whole of Life, your experience will reflect that of a human being who is separate from God, or separate from their True Self.*

All of this is just noise in the mind that you believe to be true, and since you believe it, it becomes your experience. However, Awakening doesn't have anything to do with belief or action, it has to do with seeing clearly. You could be the most uncoordinated human Being and still discover your highest Self, but you can see how one might carry the assumption that Enlightened beings are all coordinated to the fullest.

In your journey of letting go of the nonsense in your mind, you will also find it necessary to let go of the ideas that say what Awakening will or will not be iike for you. If you are determined to know what will happen, you only restrict the flow by trying to know the unknown. This goes back to wanting to be in control, but that which wants to be in control is just another ego that wants to protect its ideas about itself.

It is kind of like saying... I don't want to Awaken if it means I won't be able to follow my aspirations. This, of course, is to say that my wellness or wholeness comes from my fanciful dream or expectation, which again lives in the non-existent tomorrow. Since what you're looking for in your dream is wholeness and fulfillment, let go of the fanciful dream and be fulfilled *now*, where you are.

As you become a servant to Life rather than your ego, it becomes quite clear that it really doesn't matter what you do or don't do or what happens or doesn't happen. What does matter is that you are here, in this moment. This is very difficult to accept if you still deeply believe something outside you can make your being well again.

All you must do is look at your past experiences. Haven't you ever wanted something so, so, so badly, and then after having acquired it, you realized that it wasn't such a big deal? Or better yet, after you failed miserably and didn't get what you so desperately wanted, you discovered that everything was just fine.

To be bound by such movement in the mind is to become a slave to an imaginary world; a world in which suffering is relieved through getting what you want, even though that hasn't worked yet.

Living for the ego is the predominant motivation for the vast majority of human beings; by vast majority I mean upwards of ninety nine percent. Remember, this isn't to say that it is wrong, but is to merely point to a confusion of being. If you move on behalf of the ego, believing it to be true, you tell the universe to treat you as you perceive yourself to be.

There is a slippery slope here; you might tend to believe that if you just think about being whole with life, this will align you with your True Self. This isn't what I'm pointing to. If this is done, you may find yourself in a fight against your mind or your ego. You may try to repress or manipulate thought, and this is a form of resistance, as you believe the negative thought should be something other than what it is.

If you would like to see the negative thoughts fall away, all you must do is stop energizing those thoughts with your attention. You give them attention because you believe them to be true, and you become afraid of their content. By now, I hope you are beginning to see how no thought is true, and the more you question the thought rather than pushing it away, it naturally subsides.

If you run from negative thought to positive thought, you proclaim that negative thought is to be feared, which only solidifies your reality where negative thoughts can harm you.

You can see these negative movements in the mind as a gift as they point to the delusion you hang on to. See their presence as a blessing, for they serve as the perfect teacher, pointing you to the delusion in your mind that creates limitation. If you attempt to push thought away, you are acknowledging that you see it as a threat, which is only to validate its existence, making them stronger or more prominent in your life.

When you question thought rather than react to thought, you position *yourself* as the master of the mind, instead of allowing the mind to be your master. In this space of questioning, insight and wisdom are what flows through us, rather than a fear that only generates a knee jerk reaction that goes nowhere.

If your True Self is what you are already, there is nothing you must do to get back to Self. You must only allow that which obstructs your vision to fall away, which happens through questioning your perception. Most of the time people want to cultivate positive thoughts because they don't want their negative thoughts to define them; they want to move from a negative thinking ego, to a positive thinking ego.

Such a thing can improve the relative quality of your life for sure. However, this is not where your liberation is. You can become a slave to positive thoughts just as easily as you become a slave to the negative ones. The invitation is to wake up from the mental prison all together, in doing so your natural and True Self emerges as the motivation that moves you. In this you will discover your thoughts naturally become more loving, without any effort on your part.

> **When you question thought rather than react to thought, you position yourself as the master of the mind, instead of allowing the mind to be your master.**

There is no freedom from ego, but only the freedom to not be a slave to ego. Ego has a right to be, and you only become a slave to it when you believe it to actually define you.

As you live your life, see if you can notice this movement that wants to serve the ego. If you make a decision, are you doing so with intent to serve your mentally created self-image? If you buy something, are you doing so with the hope of adding value to your ego? When you help someone, do you only do it because you're trying to build up this mental dream with the hope that others might approve of you?

It might be a good point to address this concept of self-image, which in most cases is just another name for an ego. We've spent tremendous amounts of energy trying to help people and ourselves to build a strong and healthy self-image. But what is this image? It is simply another creation of the mind, with the hope that a positive ego rather than a negative one can be created.

Yes, such a thing can be helpful as it pertains to living a relatively happier life, but again, I'm not here to teach you how you can trick yourself into being happy. The intent is to wake up to a beauty that is *already* here. To try and create a positive self-image is a mental game, which has nothing to do with what you actually are.

If you believe the positive thoughts about your mentally created image, then by default you believe that thought itself as true, setting yourself up to be deceived by the mind. What happens here is you find yourself in a reactive game that is constantly trying to uphold this self-image. Doing so, keeps you as a prisoner to the mind, albeit maybe a happier prisoner, but a prisoner nonetheless.

You still find yourself engaged in unwanted mental acrobatics, and needlessly suffering over mental content that simply isn't true. The point I'm making is to let go of all mental images of who you think you are or more accurately, to see through them; see how each mental image has no real substance as it pertains to your True identity.

> *To try and create a positive self-image is a mental game, which has nothing to do with what you actually are.*

Chapter 10
Freedom

The word "Freedom" has just as many diverse meanings as there are as many diverse people walking on the Earth. In the sense that I use this word, I am pointing to the experience of being unbounded by whatever arises in each moment.

Freedom, from a collective sense, would probably be seen as an external happening that is given by another person or institution. This, of course, proclaims that the experience of Freedom is dictated by something outside you. This freedom is most commonly used as a tool of manipulation, as the one who extends such freedom can threaten to take it away.

I would suggest that you give up relying on all forms of external freedom to create a sense of wellness within your being. Clinging to this external freedom reinforces the egoistic self that is separate from your inherent Freedom.

There is an infectious thought spread through the consciousness of humankind that says your wellness as a human being is determined by your external conditions. If this was true, than those with more resources would automatically be free of suffering, or experience a life with a greater sense of well-being; this simply and clearly is not true.

If you say that you know this deeply, yet still find yourself looking to external conditions to feel whole and complete, you only deceive yourself. To be dishonest about such a thing is to say that you feel unworthy to find out that you seek something outside of yourself. This again is looking for self-worth in the mind.

If you buy into the false freedom brought on by a collective worldview, you will only find yourself as a pawn serving the egoistic needs of other people and delaying your own Awakening.

I heard once that Freedom is not "freedom from" anything, but more appropriately stated, it is "freedom to." Are you free enough to be what you are in this moment, or do you find yourself resisting this moment as if your freedom was in some other moment?

If sadness arises, are you free enough to feel sad? If joy arises, are you free enough to feel joy? The only reason you restrict such happenings within you is because you believe the delusion that says you are unworthy if you feel how you feel. This only presents judgment on your emotions rather than embracing them. By judging or resisting them in your mind, you miss the lesson that wants to shine through.

Every experience you have is meant to serve your Awakening, which arises with the intention to show you something valuable. If you live your life with a constant rejection of these emotions you close the door to the movement of Life that is trying to support you.

Who cares if other people accept your experience or not, it's irrelevant. Just as your thoughts about someone else crying has nothing to do with their genuine unfolding. Other people's thoughts about you are not true, but only a reflection of how they feel about such a movement within themselves.

The challenge here might be that you still believe that other people's acceptance of you, determines how your life will unfold. For most, this is a delusion that goes back to childhood, as you have been conditioned to believe that other people's approval of you is vital for your life experience to flourish. The only thing I can say about that is... so how's that working out so far?

The mental insanities that I point to are for most people deeply ingrained. Have compassion for yourself in knowing that mental movement or conditioning doesn't define your worth, but rather you are already worthy of Life before the mind moves.

Genuine Freedom points to absolute acceptance; and the experience of this Freedom within yourself is likened to the internal sensation of being absolutely accepted as you are now in this moment and every other moment. Can you get a sense of this?

You only need to look at your constant mental movement that seeks to become accepted or approved of. The energy of this can quite sincerely become exhausting, as you find yourself chasing something that can never be pinned down.

The only way to fully embody this Freedom that I point to is by extending it to all of life. What I mean by this is that if you desire the experience of Freedom, Acceptance, and Explosive Love, then you must be willing to share this with the whole of Life.

It's one thing to *say* you extend Freedom, and it's another thing to actually *do* it, and it isn't so much about the actual doing of it as it is about *seeing* it within yourself. For when it is seen clearly as your natural state of being, it will be as if you have no other option than to share such Beauty with the world.

So again, let us not get caught up in what you should do nor should not do, but focus still on seeing Reality clearly.

Notice the resistance within your own life experience to see if you actually are extending Freedom. If you feel as though there is a fight within you or some argument with Reality, it is a clear indication that you are withholding this Love.

> *If one desires the experience of Freedom, Acceptance, and Explosive Love, then you must be willing to share this with the whole of Life.*

This is a good time to bring up the issue of compounding your delusion. This means that you feel your internal resistance and add to it by not accepting or Loving the resistance you hold. The point being that it is to not rid yourself of anything, but merely to be aware of what is happening. If you resist your resistance, you only strengthen the resistance you are carrying.

For example, when you get angry with someone, and you take on a spiritual ego that says this isn't right, therefore, you mustn't be angry. Thus, this throws you back into the game of judgments, restricting the flow of clarity that wants to show you what is True. So here you have resistance manifesting as anger, and then you've compounded the resistance by condemning your anger.

I'm not suggesting that all of a sudden you'll enter into this space of Freedom and never return to the current mental delusion that might seem so prevalent in your life now. What I am suggesting, though, is as you engage in this process or practice of Awareness, you find that your mental clinging becomes less and less.

As you move into this Freedom, it won't matter so much that it doesn't happen all of a sudden, since you will notice the progress being made, seeing clearly how you are moving into a more Awake way of living.

In each moment that you find to be uncomfortable or disheartening, ask yourself if you are free enough to feel what is happening right now.

If you find that you are not, ask yourself if you are free enough to run from it; if that's what you find yourself doing. There is no room for compounded self-condemnation. As you step back and question your inherent Freedom, you might notice that what is created is a more open space for each moment to unfold.

When you step back and question the mind's content, you automatically become less identified with the thought that passes through the mind. This is because you give yourself permission not to react to the mind with a conditioned response, but rather create an openness within you that allows for greater clarity to be seen.

Chapter 11
The Unknown

It's common to assume that the one who is Awake must know something that the asleep being does not know. In this assumption, you engage the quest to acquire knowledge that will lead you to Awakening. To be quite direct, this movement of trying to attain something with the hope of becoming Enlightened, be it certainty or knowledge, is a quest that leads you away from your most natural unfolding.

The Awake being is Awake not because they know something in the mind; the Awake being is Awake because they rest in the Truth that knows they know nothing. This points to the challenge of using information or words to help one see their True nature. The trap is that the one, who is searching, will use the information as a tool to solidify that they know something.

You then can fall prey to the ridiculous movement of trying to convince others of what you know and find ways to prove how what others know is not true. This isn't Awake living; this is the same old game you've played your whole life of looking to the mind as a source of sustenance, just dressed in different clothing.

It might help to bring clarity by sharing a poem.

Knowing

Can I be honest,
even though I might Cry?
I really, truly, deeply don't know what I want.
...and sometimes, yes, I wish I could fly.

How could this be,
for the One who writes so poetically?
The One who seems so sure,
as he dances with Life so Confidently.

Then dear One, you are mistaken.
My wholeness does not come
with knowing tomorrow.
My freedom does not live
at the end of Desire's road,
My Liberation is in my Honesty,
When I fully admit that 1 don't really know.

I don't know what tomorrow holds;
I don't know which stones to throw.
I don't know who's right and who's wrong,
I only know that I am here, in this moment alone.

I don't know what should or should not happen.
I don't know the next line of this Poem.
But somehow when I give up trying,

Life unfolds and ends up rhyming,
Always bringing me back home.

My strength is in not knowing,
Not obsessing about knowing the unknown.
For who really knows tomorrow?
Who can go back and change yesterday's sorrow?

So I sit, Patiently.
Realizing that beyond now,
I know nothing.
I let go of the dream that thinks it knows,
the imaginary self
that wants to become a somebody.

I melt, in this moment
Where Life is real and true.
It is this space where freedom Lives,
and I see nothing but Love in me and you.

My favorite sentence in this poem is, *"My strength is in not knowing, Not obsessing about knowing the unknown."*

If you were to see clearly, you would notice that the mental noise that seems to bring about so much unwanted movement is really an effort to know the unknown, to know that which can never be known.

You have become confused by believing that security or stability comes by way of knowing something or being sure of something. You tell stories in the mind that you look to, with the hope that you can feel secure.

The Truth, however, is that you don't really know tomorrow and you don't really know what should or should not be. The effort to trick yourself into knowing something, only leads you to the attempt to manipulate life so it conforms to the stories in your mind.

If life shows itself to not be in alignment with your stories, you become afraid as it threatens your perceived security, and you respond with stress, anxiety, etc. This is as I've stated already, relying on the content in the mind rather than relying on the Truth of Reality. This reverts back to being so desperate in getting what you want; as you think that by getting what you want will be the answer to all your problems.

You are invited to watch this mental movement in your own life experience. Do you see yourself stressing about knowing that which can never be known? Do you see yourself wanting so desperately to know what is right and what is wrong, who is good and who is bad?

As you engage these thoughts as if they were seeking something that is true, you empower them, and by empowering them you allow the thoughts to overtake you.

> *The Awake being is Awake not because they know something in the mind; the Awake being is Awake because they rest in the Truth that knows they know nothing.*

It's a common concern to wonder how one could ever live in this space of the unknown. How could you ever live life fully by admitting that you know nothing beyond this moment? Well, the point isn't that you do nothing because you know nothing; the point is that you don't *attach* yourself to what it is you only think you know. You don't look to your false knowing as a source of well-being.

This creates an open space in your being for Life itself to move rather than relying on the movement in your mind. So it's not to say that you don't make plans for tomorrow, you simply don't look to those plans as a means of identifying yourself.

> *The point isn't that you do nothing because you know nothing; the point is that you don't attach yourself to what it is you only think you know.*

For example, you plan on getting a new job, but you don't look to the fulfillment of that plan to determine your worth. If the job doesn't work out, there is a recognition that says it simply wasn't meant to be at that particular time; and there must be something else that life is trying to do to support your movement as a human being; you simply do not know what that is yet.

If a plan doesn't work out and it bothers you internally, it can only be due to the fact that you are looking to the outcome to define who you think you are. The wonderful news of which is that you can allow this discomfort to be a signal rather than a threat. In seeing the discomfort as an alarm going off that wants to show you a deeper Truth, you immediately become less bothered by the discomfort as you find yourself embracing it rather than trying to push it away.

Knowing tomorrow or knowing something that you don't know now, has nothing to do with living peacefully in this moment. It is as if you are trying to set yourself up to live peacefully tomorrow while you live with stress today. How silly.

The fullness of living Awake comes by way of trusting the unknown; by trusting that Life will unfold in the way that Life sees fit, rather than how the mind sees fit. This becomes quite easy once you see the fallacy in trusting the mind, or in trusting thought that can never be true.

Imagine yourself traveling on a path that takes you through a dense forest. As you enter into this forest you notice a curious thing, there seems to be a tremendous amount of chaos, trees that have fallen, dead branches everywhere, vines and bushes seemingly out of place. One could look at this life condition and tell a story about how this environment is wrong or unorganized.

Quite sincerely, one could freak out and fall to their knees as they see something that is perceived to be a huge mess, a huge problem. Is it true though? Is it true that the trees should not be lying on the ground rotting, or that branches should not have fallen where they have?

If you look at your favorite neighborhood lawn, you'll notice how it doesn't resemble "Life" per se, but it resembles the mind's idea of order and organization. Because you know where everything is, and because the grass is separated from the rocks, you can seemingly define everything and put it into a category, which then allows you to feel safe.

I find it quite hilarious that if you let the lawn go unattended for too long, life doesn't give two shits about your idea of order and organization. Life does what it does to support Life as a whole, it doesn't care about the separation you've created in your mind, nor does it care about the separate self you've created in your mind; for it knows it as *not* true, but only a dream.

Just as in watching the seasons change, life doesn't care if you like rain or not, if life moves the clouds to produce rain, it does so because it is necessary to support all of life. Your argument with its movement does nothing but restrict your own existence, your own flow of Love. If you embrace the rain, if you embrace life as it is, then you find that your restrictive arguments fall away.

In this forest I spoke about, the perceived chaos is not really chaotic. Every leaf that falls does so intentionally; every dead branch serves as a vital role to help life continue to go on. Every changing of the seasons is not there to please your ego, but happens so that life might continue on. Just as every fallen tree supports Life's infinite unfolding, every life experience that presents itself is there to support your own infinite unfolding.

If you were to proclaim that the seasons should not be as they are, and you could somehow only keep the summer time, disregarding fall, winter, and spring; what would happen? Everything would dry out and die, in a relative sense. Just as in your own life, if you proclaim that happy times are the only valuable times and you removed any sadness from the human experience, you would be setting yourself up for the same kind of disaster.

The difficulties in living with the seasons are not the seasons themselves, but your internal resistance to the seasons, or your arguments. Because you want so badly for life to be something other than what it is, internally you restrict the flow of Life; you are trying to swim upstream rather than flowing *with* the movement of Life.

The reason a seemingly chaotic forest might not bother you so much is that you are not looking at the forest to tell you who you are. For the lawn example though, imagine you have the most perfect lawn and a herd of buffalo come raging through your most prized accomplishment.

Yeah, you might be a little pissed off.

Why? Because you look at this accomplishment to define who you are; when the accomplishment becomes threatened you feel as though who you are is being threatened and respond with fear. Again, it is a fear of losing something that isn't even real though, a self that is defined by thought.

Can you see how this lesson might help in bringing healing to your past? Just as in the forest example, what seems to be wrong, misplaced, or out of sync is not the forest itself, but it is your thoughts about the forest. What hurts in your life, are not the events, but your stories *about* those events. You tell mind generated stories that seemingly determine your value, and believe that the stories about the events are true; therefore there is an internal response as if the thoughts were true.

> *Just as every fallen tree supports Life's infinite unfolding, every life experience that presents itself is there to support your own infinite unfolding.*

Most people are haunted by their past simply because they believe in the stories that they tell, especially believing the stories of being a victim. That story is so deeply believed that defensiveness is at the forefront if someone even *suggests* that the story of the past isn't true. These stories are held onto so tightly because you look at them to define who you are, even if those stories create nothing but suffering. To give up the story, or lay it down is to lay down who you think you are, which can seem to leave you incredibly vulnerable and open, which scares most people.

This isn't to suggest that the past never happened; but is to suggest that your interpretation of the past is not true. Just like, if ten people stared up at the clouds and gave their interpretation of what the clouds looked like, there may very easily be ten different interpretations. Which one is true though?

What *is* True is that Life is as it is; the clouds are as they are, and this is independent of your thoughts about them. To label some as good and some as bad is not to define them but only to expose your own conditioning, your own fears. Just as in your past experiences, to say some are good and some are bad is only to show what you've been conditioned to believe are good and bad, having nothing to do with what is actually True.

At first, it might seem to be a difficult thing to look at the past and let go of your story. This is fine. The difficulty shows you how blinded you've become by believing your story. Remember, there is no goal that says you must let go; for letting go happens on its own. You must only be willing to see how these stories are not true, and in their own time they will fall away naturally and without effort.

Just as in observing the forest, you don't have to become bothered by its presence since you can see how it is all working out for the common good of Life, so that Life might continue on. You can trust that the forest is right where it needs to be, even if you don't understand the how or why. Trusting the unknown allows you to enjoy your stroll through the forest without getting caught up in the mental game of trying to define whether or not it's right or wrong.

This same trust is waiting to be seen, as it relates to your past. Can you trust that the events of the past are not there to define you, but rather to show you your own depth and the Loving depth of Life? Can you rest in the unknown? Can you accept that even though you don't know how or why things have happened, Life is doing what needs to be done to allow it to continue on?

Very quickly you might find yourself drumming up all sorts of questions with the hope of understanding why it is that violence happens, or why people hurt each other, and how it is that this is helpful for life to unfold.

I could write until my fingers fall off attempting to explain such a thing, but really nothing would be explained at all. An answer could be provided, and then given enough time another question would present itself that seems to threaten an answer that once seemed to suffice. This is the never-ending quest of the mind to find security; a quest that quite sincerely goes nowhere. It is an infinite loop that could keep you searching your whole life.

I'm not suggesting that these questions are without value, but I'm just implying that the answers to your questions are not the key to Awakening. As Love continues to Explode within you, by seeing Life with more clarity, these answers or insights will present themselves in ways that are beyond my ability to explain them to you.

> *Can you accept that even though you don't know how or why things have happened, Life is doing what needs to be done to allow it to continue on?*

I would much rather see you trust in your own insight rather than looking to the insight I share as your source of wisdom. This, of course, is the point... To have you stand on your own authority.

You have these questions in your mind that seem so important, resulting in you building a fortress around them, as if you can't Awaken or let go, until this "one" question gets answered.

This, of course, again, is to say that your liberation lives in the mind. It reminds me of a poem from my previously referenced book.

Spiritual Cancer

What is this heart ache of
believing you are without?
What is this nonsense
of being surrounded by doubt?

Is it the sensation
of clinging to just one more answer?
Do we not know,
this is the source of our spiritual cancer?

If our prayers were answered,
would we then believe that all will be well?
Only for a moment, a second,
until more pain began to swell.

How many times
have you passed through this gate of illusion?
Believing for one more "thing,"
to cure the inner confusion.

When we can release this idea
that there is truth in the "have not,"
Surely we will discover a joy in life
that's present and cannot be bought.

There is nothing you can gain;

no prize, no recognition.
There is no-thing you are without,
not even a single ambition.

Find freedom from want,
by "being" what you desire.
Allow life as it is now,
to be that which can inspire.

Do you not know
that you have all that is needed?
Allow it to grow my friend,
it has already been seeded.

This egoistic quest of finding answers is to proclaim that you are un-whole in this moment. The search itself is to try to move from the unknown to the known, which is an impossible task as it relates to anything beyond this moment. Can you stop searching for wholeness? Can you stop trying to find yourself by knowing something that cannot be known in the mind?

To trust in the unknown is to give up your desperate wanting. For you desperately want only because you believe that the fulfillment of your want will cure your suffering. Has it worked yet?

To anxiously want something that is not real is to argue with Reality. It is to say that I am not whole and cannot be at peace until such and such happens. One of the most profound happenings upon Awakening is this release of wanting what is not. What you discover with great clarity is that you want whatever is showing, for there is a deep recognition that whatever is showing is exactly what is needed for wholeness to be embodied.

To clarify, this "wanting" that I speak of is not your preference, but is your effort to manipulate life in order to be better or to become more whole. Your preferences are a very different movement, which I'll explain.

Preference is a detached desire. This means that you may follow what you feel moved to experience without letting the outcome define who you are. If I go into an ice cream shop with chocolate on my mind, and discover they are currently out of stock of all things chocolate, it doesn't disrupt my well-being. I might simply find myself choosing a different flavor or visiting a different ice cream shop.

If I find myself getting pissed off at the lack of their ice cream selection, I'm proclaiming that my wellness is determined by the fulfillment of my desire. If I don't get what I want, I am somehow less valid, or less whole.

This presents a tremendous opportunity to look at your own experiences and see how it is you are creating your own suffering.

Can you tell the difference between your attached desires and unattached desires; or your preferences and wants? Can you see how clinging to your wants does nothing but create suffering? Are you willing to even look?

There is another trap here. You can look at your desires and see that you are attached, and then automatically assume that these desires are bad or should not be there. This isn't what I'm pointing to. Very often, a preference or a desire arises from within, which starts out as an unattached expression of Life, but as this expression reaches your mind you create an identity out of it and it then becomes an attached desire.

> **Can you see how clinging to your wants does nothing but create suffering?**

For example, say you feel moved to try out a new career. First, it is simply a preference or something that seems like it would be an enjoyable experience for your being, and then you find yourself engaged in the mental insanity of using this desire to support your mentally created self. You say that the fulfillment of this desire will make you a more lovable or acceptable person, and in this you cling to it with the hope that it will free you from the suffering you live with.

The truth of the matter is that the fulfillment of the desire still remains in the unknown. You don't know if it will happen or not, you only know that in this moment the desire exists. It might be helpful to know that what makes the fulfillment of desire so difficult is your attachment to it.

Occasionally, you may have the experience where you find some things can be created in your life with great ease, while the seemingly most important things you desire still prove to be a challenge to create. Did it ever occur to you that the difficulty stems from you moving toward those seemingly important desires from a place of ego or separation? Because you separate yourself from the wholeness of Life, you find that your journey is only met with resistance.

Resting in the unknown is to acknowledge that you don't know if your desires should or should not be fulfilled. Perhaps, the case is that you are only meant to move in this direction for short time, and that this short path might be trying to show you something deeper than just the fulfillment of desire. However, if you are caught up and attached to the outcome, you turn away from such a lesson and completely miss the point of the desire in the first place.

It is just like a baby who discovers that it could crawl, but then it gets caught up in the identity of the one who only crawls. And in the process, not realizing that this movement of crawling was only meant to be a temporary experience that led to a more productive way of experiencing life as one who walks and runs.

The one who is attached to crawling might find that at thirty years old they are still crawling, as they have impressed on their identity as one who has mastered crawling. The pride in their identity only blinds them to a deeper way of living.

Your efforts to hold on to what you think you know, only blinds you to a much deeper knowing or unfolding.

As your perception becomes clearer in seeing that your internal discomfort is not created by the external world, you can ask yourself with great sincerity... is it true that being sure about tomorrow will reduce my suffering? You see, you play a game in your mind that constantly searches for a security that will never be there.

Just as someone searches for security through monetary gain, they have the thought, if only I had fifty thousand dollars in the bank, I could be relaxed. Or to another, it's only five thousand dollars, and yet to another it can be five million. The point is that it's not the external condition, but your thoughts about what it means to have such and such amount of money in the bank.

This can also unfold as believing if a certain political figure gets elected then you can calm down and finally rest. One person might believe if candidate A gets elected all is going to go to hell, but for another if candidate A gets elected then everything is going to be just fine. Do you see the insanity here?

Yes, it might be tough to acknowledge that this is how you live your life; constantly searching for something that isn't real. But Dear One, please hear this, it's okay to see such things because it is through this process of seeing that allows change to take place. The more you resist this honesty in seeing how you live your life, the more you resist the Love that wants only to bring well-being to your world.

It is not to say that searching for something that is not there is wrong. We are only questioning if our movement is creating suffering, and asking sincerely, do we want to continue living a life that suffers, that chases something that is not even there, or would we rather live a life that is joyful in this moment?

I'm reminded of the saying, "Do you want to be *right*, or do you want to be *happy*?" Just as if someone gets irritated while reading this, they're more concerned with being right than they are with being happy. In Truth, even if there is zero agreement with what is being stated, by no means do you have to experience irritation simply because you are reading something that doesn't resonate with you.

It's like reading a recipe on how to make a cake; if you are not familiar with the recipe, you don't necessarily find yourself getting stressed out or irritated. You only become bothered if you believe the recipe somehow threatened who you are thought to be.

What is it that you are holding onto with the hope that it will make you well again? What are you waiting for with the hope that it will allow you to finally rest in joy? Are you waiting for someone to forgive you? Are you waiting for your body to change? Are you waiting for that promotion, or the approval from others?

Discover the rules you have in place in order to be joyful, and then throw those rules in the trash and be joyful without cause or reason. If you have reasons in place to be happy or not happy, all you are doing is creating conditional love. You are again looking to the mind to tell you if it's okay to Love; if you look to the mind to give you permission to Love, you become a slave to mental movements.

> *What is it that you are holding onto with the hope that it will make you well again?*

These reasons or conditions are only arguments that are based on nothing that is true, but rather are based on your conditioning. As you step back and question these conditions with a humble heart, you will see how they only create limits rather than freedom.

These reasons or conditions are a mental effort to create security, or to know the unknown. Many of these thoughts you cling to are thoughts you've clung to your whole life. Because of this, the thought of letting them go is like letting go of everything you hold dear. So be of good cheers in seeing the suffering that wants to hold on to them; have compassion for the mind because it honestly believes it is doing a good thing in its holding on. However, the mind is just confused about what it's actually doing, and what is actually true.

Similarly, if a child believes so strongly that there is a monster hiding in the closet, you wouldn't be so quick to condemn the child, but would have compassion in knowing that the fear was only imaginary, knowing that the child really is fine, and only confused about what is real.

Even if you find yourself to "lose it" emotionally as you begin to see more clearly, it won't be seen as such a big deal, but rather an innocent movement of your being that is just confused a tiny bit. Often you will find yourself laughing at these outbursts because you find that they do not threaten you so much anymore, but rather you embrace them as wonderful, life unfolding opportunities.

Rest in the unknown, fully admit to yourself that what you *think* to be true is only a movement in the mind that isn't really true, but rather is only a movement of conditioning. Don't simply acknowledge it because you are told to; acknowledge it by seeing clearly the Truth of Reality.

Chapter 12
Relationships

The concept of relationship is my favorite subject in this book, simply for the reason that this concept or movement of relationship is going to serve as one of your greatest teachers.

Fulfilling relationships are most commonly sought after with the hope of eliminating the suffering in our lives. It is a common assumption that if we can find the perfect relationships, our internal dis-ease will subside. However, and I'm sure you see this coming, to chase such a thing, is to put your wellness outside of what you already are, creating a chase that goes nowhere.

Most people look at others who seemingly have fantastic relationships, and assume that the reason they are so happy is because they've found their perfect match. Often you can look at your own relationships and create all sorts of excuses as to why your relationship must be creating your suffering. And in this, naturally you see "relationships" as the culprit to your suffering.

To be quite clear, the most joyful relationships are not a result of two people completing each other, but rather it is a result of two people who have learned not to rely on the other person to make them whole or unwhole. The difficulties in relationships arise when one person believes the other person owes them something, or must conform to whom one or the other thinks they should be.

Investigating such a thing can sometimes be quite difficult because you have spent so much time blaming another person for your internal heartache or dis-ease. Can you move beyond this? If you are to continue this unfolding, to continue your willingness to let Love Explode within you, you must see clearly that other people are not responsible for your suffering.

It can be a challenging thing to lay down your weapons of judgment and remove the log from your own eye before trying to blame someone else, which points to the initial courage necessary to move forward.

The element that is most common in a dysfunctional relationship is the element of blame, or believing that someone else is responsible for your suffering. If you insist on holding onto to such insanity, you will simply never Awaken. Not because life doesn't want you to, but because of your own stubbornness in not being willing to let go. You may even find it helpful to just accept the *possibility* that another person is *not* responsible for your suffering; this might create the space needed to see clearly.

Let's look at an example of a married couple who seem to be surrounded by conflict. Let's say the husband is quite upset because his wife or significant other is not getting a job, or won't look for a job in the manner that the husband sees as appropriate.

If the husband gets upset about the non-action of his spouse, what he is proclaiming is that his wellness is determined by the actions of another person. In addition to this, what the husband might also proclaim is that his well-being or security is threatened by the non-action of another. Since this is the perception of the husband, life will move to support what is being projected. This means that the husband will experience scarcity or limitation because he believes that his source of sustenance is threatened by an external circumstance.

What is really being threatened though? If you believe the mind's content, you will believe that what the mind points out as being threatened is actually true. However, if you step back, you may be able to see that what is really being threatened is the false identity that has been created in the mind and what you are really afraid of losing is this false identity.

For example, the husband wants to see himself as a "standup" guy who has a household income that affords him the ability to maintain who he is thought to be. If he sees his wife as not contributing enough, then this idea of self becomes threatened. And in the same manner, as you become afraid of losing who you are thought to be, you respond with a fear that might manifest as anger directed towards your partner; as you mistakenly see your partner as the one who is responsible for your perceived loss.

In Truth though, the conflict is not a result of the spouse not getting a job, but rather a result of the husband not seeing Reality clearly. If the husband began to realize that his spouse was not responsible for his suffering, he might step back and investigate his own movement rather than blaming someone else.

The challenge, of course, is that most people simply do not understand or see clearly enough to notice that the conflict is created from within, and not without. The more you hold on to your blaming, the more you become blinded to the Truth that's waiting to shine through. It isn't enough to simply say, "Okay, I don't blame them." This is really a deep internal acknowledgment that takes place in the heart.

This is why it does no good to just say, "I don't blame," when in truth you hide the blame deep within you. It doesn't matter what you say, but what matters is the condition of your heart. For this reason there is no hiding allowed as it pertains to Awakening; Life knows if you're not being honest and Life knows if you hide judgment in your heart, just as you really know. You can hide from others, but you cannot hide from your True Self.

The major hang up in relationships stem from all the preconceived ideas you have as you enter into relationships. You meet someone, and in your mind you create an idea of who they are or who they *should* be, and in hanging on to those ideas so tightly, the moment those ideas of who you *think* they are becomes threatened, you freak out and become fearful. You are looking to your ideas about others to make you whole, rather than simply enjoying the other person as they truly are.

If you enter into a relationship with hopeful expectations, than you are quite sincerely setting yourself up for disappointment. Relationship drama only occurs when you hold onto expectation as if the fulfillment of your expectation would somehow create wholeness in your life. Again, proclaiming that your wholeness lives in some event in the future outside yourself.

You may ask... "Hopeful expectations in what sense?" What I mean is, believing that the relationship should be something other than or better than what it is right now. This comes back to attempting to know the unknowable. Is it true that your relationship will be better than what it is now? Such a thing can never be known, simply by the fact that the idea of "better," is a relative idea just like "good or bad," and it doesn't really exist.

The only thing that would happen if the relationship did become "better," would be that your thoughts *about* the relationship would seem to be better. So your experience of a bad relationship or a good one has nothing to do with the *actual* relationship and has everything to do with your *thoughts about* that relationship.

The dilemma here is that people have fallen in love with their thoughts *about* others, rather than falling in Love with the *reality* of others. You've most likely spent your whole life believing that you either love someone or you hate them, but in truth what you love or hate is really your *thoughts about them* which has nothing to do with what or who they really are.

> *The difficulties in relationships arise when one person believes the other person owes them something.*

What I am pointing to over and over again is the importance of bringing your attention to the most important relationship in your life, and that is the relationship with the Self, your True Self. This can also be stated as your relationship with Life as a Whole. Most people think their most important relationship has to do with another person, as they think the fulfillment of this relationship will somehow create the wholeness they are desperately searching for.

However, as you see, the wholeness that you search for can only be experienced from within what you are, which has nothing to do with *other* people. The role that others will play in you Awakening to your most profound relationship with the Self is that others may serve as a pointer, or even portray the role of a silent helper.

What this means is that your close relationships help you to create a safe space where you can be honest and loving, which are key elements to help you to lay down the weapons that obstruct your vision. Often, this is seen playing out in deep friendships more so than in marriages. In friendships there is typically less on the line, because you are not looking so much for your friends to conform to who you think they should be, rather you would prefer to just enjoy their company.

This isn't to say that friendships are always free of conflict but just to say that friendships can sometimes be more constructive because you have less attachment to them. In marriage, people often hold the assumption that they must be together for the rest of their lives. With this belief comes the fear that life will be miserable unless someone outside you changes or stays the same; again believing that the external world is responsible for your well-being.

In addition to this, even the close relationships that seem to be ripe with drama, like with your mother or father, brother or sister, also help to point out the internal insanity, as they draw to the surface many insecurities and expectations we cling to.

There are numerous examples we could go over to show how it is you create suffering for yourself in relationships. Rather than relying on me to explain them, I encourage you to take this issue of seeing clearly serious enough to where you practice seeing clearly on your own. Are you willing to be still and question the validity of the arguments you hold onto?

Truthfully, throughout this whole book I'm only repeating myself in a thousand different ways. Essentially what I am saying is You are what You search for. There is nothing outside this moment or in the external world that can bring healing to your soul. Stop looking to the external and wake up to the wholeness you've always been, always are and always will be.

We are treading in dangerous water here. I know that much of the content in this book can be met with passionate disagreement or down right accusal that what I am saying is careless and harmful. Yes, it is dangerous, but so is a hammer if used incorrectly.

The insights in this book are like anything else, if not used for its intended purposes it can create confusion or harm. However, if you become agitated by this content, what is being seen is not my Heart's True intent, but rather your own insistence on validating how important you think you are.

It would be easy to assume that because I talk about a certain type of relationship to be delusional; that in some way I'm implying that it is wrong or should not be. Let me be clear by saying that a delusional idea about relationships is no more valuable than a relationship that is free of delusion. No matter what relationship you may find yourself in, every experience that presents itself is of equal value, as every experience presents itself as a teacher to lead you to a more profound way of experiencing Life.

Another example of relationship conflict that might arise is holding onto resentment with the hope that the person you're condemning owns up to and accepts the idea that they wronged you. Let's say a wife is lying in bed, holding onto frustration and anger toward her partner because he didn't do something that she thought he should.

As she lays there in bed, her blood begins to boil as she energizes every thought that reinforces why he was wrong.

One thought after another serves as confirmation as to why she is right and he is wrong. During this whole process, the wife feels restricted as she consciously withholds love from her partner.

Where is the Love really being withheld?

Yes... since the wife wants to hold onto her arguments she ignores any loving movement that might want to arise within her. She feels that because she is withholding Love, she is doing a good service by showing in her actions or thoughts that what he did was wrong. This is done with an intent to protect the love within her, but because the love is misguided or confused, and believed to be created by the external, all she really does is withhold Love from herself.

If she was to drop these arguments and allow her emotions to unfold naturally, they would serve as a teacher that wants to show her the error in her perception. Since dropping the argument is not an option for her, due to her fear that she might be proven wrong or invalid, she grips tightly to her frustration.

This, again, is done with an effort to protect who you are *thought* to be, which has nothing to do with your partner but everything to do with your own insecurities.

Even if you don't agree with what your partner does, is it true that life should not have unfolded that way? Can you say for certain that you know what is best for another human being? If a tree falls on your house, can you say for certain that it was wrong? Does life even care about what you *think*?

Your inability to accept or to extend love towards another person because of their actions is really an effort to reinforce the non-acceptance of your own actions. If there are things in your past that you still look at as wrong, invalid, or unacceptably negative, you will by default point out the wrong actions of others with the intent to prove your own self as unworthy.

Let this be a wonderful unfolding though, for when you have difficulty in extending freedom to others, it is a clear sign that you are not extending freedom to yourself. This is the beauty in relationships, for they serve as a most wonderful teacher in showing you how you create limitation for your own life experience.

As you get close to another human being, you get closer to yourself. This is not because the other human being completes you, but because you let your guard down, exposing your True Self. As you tend to accept those you Love, you create a space within this acceptance that allows you to accept yourself more. In doing so, you become more open to the Love that wants to explode within you.

A nice illustration here is to touch on the subject of lovemaking or sex. For the one who has experienced a very deep and intimate sexual connection with another human being, this example will shed light on some amazing insight.

Did you ever notice that it is very difficult to engage in a deeply wonderful sexual experience if you are caught up in the emotional drama playing out in your mind? Better yet, can you see the difficulty in engaging in such a thing if you're totally insecure about your body? The more uncomfortable you are with yourself, the more difficult it is to let go and allow yourself to fall into the pleasure of the moment.

It's kind of like getting a massage; if you are insecure about your stomach, the moment someone touches your stomach you tense up and become anxious, as if you are about to be found out or exposed.

What is happening here?

The moment you experience insecurity, you start believing mental content that is caught up in dualistic thought. You believe the thoughts that say you are too fat or too small, too much or not enough. As you get caught up in this mental dream, you move away from the moment and start serving an imaginary world that lives in the mind.

To melt into the arms of another person, you must be willing to lay down these thoughts that tell you that you are unwhole. Often the reason it feels so good to fall into the arms of a loved one is because you experience acceptance; you feel as though this person isn't judging you. Therefore, it is safe to be vulnerable and free.

The trap here, though, is believing that the love and acceptance you feel is a result of another person's love and acceptance of you. Because of this, you cling to other people as if they hold the answer to your well-being. What is really happening, though, is that you have given yourself permission to let go because you feel like you're not being judged or condemned.

Just as easily you could fall into the arms of someone who is only pretending to accept you, and because you *think* they are accepting, you open yourself up. In Truth, it has nothing to do with the other person per se, but everything to do with what is going on within you.

Just as if you came to me and said, "Tigmonk, I need to know that you accept and love me. If you did, I could go about my life with peace." So I say, "Yes dear child, I love and accept you and find you to be completely wonderful." Do you notice how this might create a wonderful smile and feeling of freedom?

The support you felt from my words really has nothing to do with me; you simply allowed yourself the freedom to experience the acceptance of yourself, but you put it outside yourself as if it came from me, or from someone else.

You do this all the time with people you care about, as you believe your well-being comes from them by believing that their thoughts about you somehow dictate your value. When you do this, you run a mouse maze where the cheese is constantly given and taken away. You move from one relationship to another, looking for someone else to accept you when the whole time Life is simply waiting for you to accept yourself.

> *The more uncomfortable you are with yourself, the more difficult it is to let go and allow yourself to fall into the pleasure of the moment.*

As you wake up to this Truth, more and more you will notice how irrelevant it is that anyone else accepts you, let alone likes you. There will be the experience of freedom on your own authority, rather than looking to others to give you what you can only give yourself: Love.

Just as in the wonderful sexual encounter, if you are to experience the fullness of the moment, the only way to do so is to be with Love in your heart. Complete acceptance. If you engage in a sexual encounter where you are doing nothing but judging your partner or yourself, you still feel restricted. Judgments are judgments, whether you place them on yourself or on others, they only restrict the flow of Love to the Self.

Even as you judge others, you are not really judging them, for the judgments serve as a tool to reinforce the judgments you've placed on yourself.

There is only one relationship, and that is the relationship you have with yourself. It seems as though there might be lots of relationships, but really they are all just a projection in your mind, and they all point back to the relationship between you and your True Self, or between You and Life.

You can have a relationship with a rock, a person, a pet, or a tree, it doesn't matter; they are all Life happenings that point back to the relationship with yourself. If you encounter a tree and find that you have arguments with that tree, such as, that tree should not be there or you think it's ugly and unworthy; really all you have done is exposed the arguments that rest within you.

If you notice a bum on the side of the road, what is the projection that takes place in your mind? Do you see the bum as less than whole, or in some way as a deficient human being? How would it feel to accept them fully as they are, in need of nothing other than what presents itself in each moment?

You see, the beauty in life is that all around you there is this lesson. At every turn there is an opportunity to discover a deeper Truth within yourself. As you look out into the world you project the relationship you have with yourself. If you see victims, it can only be because you feel yourself to be a victim in some way. If you see inadequacy, it can only be because you feel inadequate in some way. If you see Love, it can only be because you experience the Love that is within you.

In seeing this clearly, it becomes obvious that life is not an evil plot to keep you from wellness. But on the contrary, it is a wonderful expression to help you wake up to Love. The more you acknowledge this, the more you see clearly that life wants nothing but to support you, the more open you become to the movement that wants only to express Love.

Imagine yourself lying in bed with someone you love and are about to engage in a wonderful love making session. Notice how you extend to them the freedom to be who they are in this moment, blemishes and all. Notice how you feel nothing but Love for them and deep caring that knows they are wonderful regardless of the moments when you get tricked into believing otherwise.

As you extend this freedom, Loving them unconditionally, what you feel within *yourself* is the warm Love you are extending to them. Simply by extending Love, you experience it within yourself. Again, it isn't so much that you are extending it to another person, but rather you are allowing the Love within yourself to be seen and experienced.

If you are lying in bed and criticizing your partner in your mind, you probably don't feel like getting intimate. This is the same as when you criticize Life in any way; as you hold on to your arguments, you don't feel like being intimate with Life. You only feel like reinforcing why your arguments are legitimate.

It is amazing how many couples engage in sex when one partner really doesn't want to. You shame yourself into thinking that something must be wrong with you, so you do what you don't really want to do with the hope of making someone else happy. To do so is to proclaim that the other person's happiness or wellness is in you and not in them. This point really reaffirms how you believe your wellness is outside you as well.

Doing what you don't really want to do in relationships for the purpose of making someone else happy is a trap that binds you to suffering. Might it be that you do this because you want others to sacrifice their happiness in order to make you happy? You become once again, wrapped in the delusion that an experience such as happiness is something that is created by the external world.

The movement of sacrificing your own happiness in order to make someone else happy is a delusion that keeps everyone asleep. You can see from such a sacrifice how nobody wins; if two people sacrifice happiness for each other, you simply end up with two people who are miserable.

A common question you may have is how you may help your relationship partner to experience a deeper love within his or her own self? It won't happen because you sacrifice your happiness with the hope that they will be happy. To put it directly, the greatest and most straightforward way in which to help others see more Light and Love is for you to wake up to the Light and Love within yourself. Period.

Most effort to help others is done through the perception that the other person is somehow deficient in their movement as a human being, or in some way unwhole, with the *thought* that it is up to you to help them become whole. This perception is a projection that reinforces your own experience of unwholeness and as a limited self. It is a reflection of the relationship you have with yourself, therefore you try and compensate this self-imposed limitation by helping others to become more of something; when it is in fact you yourself who feels less than whole.

I understand that such a thing can seem confusing; this is okay. If one is unfamiliar with this way of seeing, the above paragraph can seem irrational.

> *The greatest and most straightforward way in which to help others see more Light and Love is for you to wake up to the Light and Love within yourself. Period.*

What it comes down to is this; if you project unwholeness onto someone else, then you are holding onto an argument that doesn't want to accept Life, by believing in the mind that there exists a better reality beyond *this* moment. If you proclaim such a thing, you experience a reality that seems deficient in some way, experiencing each moment as if the only purpose is to get to the next moment.

If you live your life in such a way, you are serving the mind's movement rather than serving reality. Again, to do so is to separate yourself from the awesome power that rests only in this moment. A good exercise here is to watch how much the mind thinks about some other moment rather than the present moment. In our thinking, it seems as though it's vitally important to have these thoughts, but upon closer inspection, these thoughts really serve no purpose other than to keep the mind/ego busy.

Because you believe your thoughts about tomorrow or yesterday to be so valuable, you chase them, bringing your attention away from this moment. Just watch how much energy you spend chasing these thoughts, watch how you think your thinking is so important. As you do this, also notice with sincerity how it isn't necessary to be so wrapped up in what you're thinking about, but rather it is only a compulsion.

Just as in your thinking about life, notice how you get caught up in your thoughts about other people. Even when you are with another person, often times your attention is not present with them in the moment, but rather your mind is preoccupied with commenting on something that has to do with the past or the future.

I'm not suggesting that you shouldn't have these thoughts, but I'm simply inviting you to observe thought and to question its' validity. Is it really necessary to be caught up in something that isn't here and now, and what are you missing out on in the moments spent chasing a dream in the mind?

As you see more clearly that the thoughts you cling to are not actually serving what is True, your belief in them subsides. You only cling to them because you are tricked into believing that they serve some vital importance. The more you see that the mental content is just noise, the more you release your grip on the mind and allow yourself to simply be here in this moment.

Just like when you get intimate with a sexual partner, being lost in the mind limits you from experiencing the depth or the pleasure of the moment. However, the arguments that you are holding onto while with another person are not *actually* True but rather are only a distraction that you *believe* to be true.

Notice how much energy you invest in worry and notice how the mind chases certain thoughts that attempt to legitimize your worrying. If you were to add up all the energy you spent worrying and compared it to actual outcomes, you would notice that this worry really wasn't necessary at all.

I will note here; as you spend mental energy worrying, the attention you give these thoughts only creates more things to worry about. This is why we see a never-ending cycle that seems to be bound to worry. It seems as though worrying serves as something important, but actually the only thing that is being served is a dream in the mind, which says that if life doesn't work out the way you think it should, you will be less than whole in some way.

A long time ago I heard a phrase that has served as a great teacher, as it pertains to worry. "If I can't do anything about it, then there is no need to worry; if I can do something about it, then there is no need to worry."

You might argue with this and say, "Well, what if what I think I can do is something that I really *can't* do?" Or, "What if what I think I *cannot* do is something that I really *can* do?" This is to miss the point entirely.

The question is not what you may or may not be able to do, but rather... what you will or will not do? If you do something about it, you do something about it, if you don't, you do not. If you do take action, this simply means that you *can* do something. If you don't take action, this simply means that you *cannot*. To worry about what you will or will not do is to fall back into the delusion that says your worth is determined by what you do or don't do.

Another point to see here is that if you are caught up in worry or caught up in a dream in the mind, you won't be open to the insight that wants to shine through in the moment at hand. You forget that Life wants to support you, and therefore, you think that it is you who must *do* something, rather than allowing Life to *move through* you.

What isn't seen is that Life knows what is best as it pertains to your Awakening. You can look at the experience of being in the flow, or those moments where doors open and Life unfolds through you, as if it is not even you that does anything, but something greater within you that moves on your behalf. This is much the same as how an artist may effortlessly paint a picture. Within the artist is the talent that has been gifted by Life and all the artist must do is be available for this gift to unfold. The same gift is within you right now, which is the gift to be your most full Self. Within this gift, there isn't a need to worry about what you should or should not say, how you should or should not be, or what you will or will not do.

> *"If I can't do anything about it, there is no need to worry; if I can do something about it, there is no need to worry."*

If you still find it difficult to trust Life in this way, it can only be due to still believing that the fulfillment of your desires will somehow make you more acceptable or lovable.

If you cannot trust that within you is a guidance system that wants to lead you home, it will be impossible for you to trust that your relationship partner is exactly where they need to be as well. In this, you will never fully be able to be with your partner, but rather will be with your thoughts *about* your partner.

Another relationship delusion that seems to create so much suffering in your life is this issue of trust. In Truth, you don't ever really trust another person. What most people place their trust in are the thoughts *about* another person, which is really an attempt to control someone rather than to extend Love to them.

I invite you to sincerely ask yourself this question, "Is the trust I place on others really an attempt to protect who I think I am, and is this trust a movement of Love, or a movement of fear?"

If you trust someone because you want a certain outcome, this is a movement of fear. For if the trust were somehow broken you would crumble internally. This internal crumbling arises because you have attached who you are thought to be, to an outcome that you are hoping for, which again is relying on the mind to find Self.

Most relationships are wrapped in a trust that secretly wants to control someone. You proclaim internally that, "I will trust you, only if you do what I think you should do." This can only be seen if you are willing to be honest with yourself; if you are not willing, you will not experience the liberation that wants to shine through. Even though it might be tough to acknowledge that you try to manipulate others in this way, it is necessary to realize this if you desire to see through your delusions.

Can you see how doing such a thing is a form of looking to the external to find well-being? I'm not saying don't do it, but am simply asking for you to take a closer look to acknowledge and see how you create your *own* suffering, rather than believing the insanity that says your suffering is a result of *someone else* not doing what *you* think they should do.

At this point, it might be common for you to get all flustered and wonder how it is you are to live Life if everything you do stems from believing something that isn't true. Yes, I'm pointing to a completely different way of Living, however, it is not you who lives, but rather it is Life that lives through You.

Your difficulty stems from believing that what you do or don't do is up to you, as if you are the one who decides how your life will unfold. If this were the case, that you are really as in charge as you think you are, you would live without suffering, without conflict.

The reason you live with so much difficulty is because you are trying to *live* Life, rather than letting Life live *through* you. If your living is spent trying to become something, then you have missed the point of living. Those who *try* to breathe are restricted in their flow; those who *allow* breath to happen naturally will flow with life as its partner, as its friend.

Trying to live life is like *trying* to breathe; it takes tremendous effort to sustain your being. Watch your natural breath breathe itself without effort and give in to this force that allows you to be here in this moment.

Wanting other people to be something other than what they are is like *trying* to control your breath. It is trying to control Life. In doing this, you miss out on the natural movement of Life and sink deeper into an asleep state that only creates suffering. Do you see this?

Take a moment to see these delusions within your perception of others. Whether it is a politician you don't like, an associate that you think is wrong, a loved one who you think is misguided, or a neighbor who you believe to be dumb and uninformed; it is all a movement to control something you were never meant to have control over. Your effort to control such a thing is really an effort to try and support your false self; the self you have created in your mind.

We do this, as we live to support an imaginary self, we proclaim that we are separate from life surrounded by limitation and then that projection becomes our experienced reality.

Can you admit fully that you don't really know; that you don't know if the politician should or should not be doing what he does; can you admit that you don't know if a loved one is misguided? Just as your life has taken twist and turns that someone else could see with judgmental eyes; your twist and turns have served in your unfolding, so give others the freedom to do the same.

I'll say it again; we only judge the movement of others because we judge our own movement so harshly. Your judgments about others really have nothing to do with them, but have everything to do with your relationship to Life. If one is willing to allow these judgments to fall away, it is like living without *trying* to breathe and we experience a life where we move with greater ease.

The mind jumps in and asks, "Well how the hell do I let these judgments go so I can experience this reality that is being pointed to?" Dear one, you do not *do* anything, which is the whole point; stop *trying* and start seeing what is already True, here and now. If I asked you to breathe, the more you try, the more difficult it becomes as breathing is what you do naturally. Judgments arise because you are trying to know the unknowable; so simply be aware of your trying to know what can't be known. As you become aware of this insanity, it will drop on its own. Just as when you stop trying to breathe, your breath happens naturally.

In your relationships with others as you notice the judgmental thoughts, ask yourself with great sincerity... is this thought True? Do I really know that life should not unfold this way, or is it only a conditioned thought pattern that is trying to support who I am thought to be?

Every external relationship is temporary. Some seem to last only five minutes, while others can last a lifetime. Either way, they all come to an end. Believing that a relationship should last longer than the moment at hand is a delusion that wants to control life. This isn't to say that the preference of desiring a relationship to last is not there, it is just to say that you don't know with certainty whether it should or not.

The value of any relationship only exists in this moment. To try getting value out of a relationship for the future is really a ploy to protect a false self that lives in the future. Can you let go of this false self and rest as whole in this moment?

If you are with someone and caught up in a dream that is trying to protect a future relationship, you become preoccupied with your expectations, as you believe the fulfillment of these expectations will ensure that the relationship will continue. As you take on this quest of securing a relationship for tomorrow, your attention is no longer in this moment, and therefore, you separate yourself from now, missing out on a deep connection with the person you are with in this moment.

We will look closer at this by using marriages as an example. Most marriages are set up for suffering simply because of the fact that they are entered into with the assumption that the other person must now stay with you for the rest of your life. With this expectation, any time your spouse does something that *seems* to threaten this outcome, you become fearful. Often, this leads to the silly behavior of trying to manipulate someone through mind games with the hope you can keep them locked into the tiny box you've placed them in.

Let's turn the table and ask these questions. What if you found yourself in a relationship that seemed to be inconsistent with a movement in your heart, and you felt very deeply that it was simply time for you to move on? How would you feel if your partner was adamant about you staying because fifteen years ago you made an emotional commitment to do something that you were never certain about to begin with?

Any time you make a commitment for the future and cling to it as if it was a certainty, you are really trying to protect who you *think* you are or whom you think you *should* be. People enter into a marriage and believe that it has now become their identity and if the relationship somehow dissolves, it becomes painful, as it seems as if it is the self that dissolves.

Please be clear, I am not bashing on the concept of marriage. I am simply pointing out how we suffer in them. The word "marriage" is like any other word, it doesn't mean anything other than the meaning you give it; not to mention that the meaning you give isn't even true, just as you label a tree as an oak tree, it doesn't define it at all, but only helps you to communicate with others.

If you proclaim that marriage is a source of security, you proclaim that your sustenance rests in an idea, which again separates you (perceivably) from Truth, from Reality. I encourage you to hold these labels loosely, with an open hand that is not hell bent on conforming life to support your labels.

Give your relationship partner the freedom to unfold in any way that life sees fit, just as you would appreciate the freedom to unfold in any way you felt led.

If one is willing to allow these judgments to fall away, it is like living without trying to breathe and we experience a life where we move with greater ease.

Did you notice that the dishonesty in relationships stem from this delusion that wants to withhold freedom from another. It is difficult to be honest with someone who is judgmental or controlling; for it is challenging to open up if all that awaits is condemnation. So if you are curious as to why your relationship partner won't be honest with you, perhaps it is because they fear condemnation.

This isn't just for the relationships between adults, but the same relationship unfolding happens with our children as well. If a child feels as though they will be condemned, honesty simply isn't an option for them. Yes, it can be said that their fear of condemnation has nothing to do with you, but rather it is their own insecurity. However, this still doesn't excuse us from seeing clearly.

To think that someone *should be* honest is just another judgment that wants to control life. Have you not had the experience where your dishonesty served as a tremendous lesson? Sometimes it is quite necessary that you experience your own dishonesty as it shows you the Light and Love that comes with being honest.

There is also the trap that creates the belief that someone else's dishonesty can affect your well-being. It isn't the dishonesty of others that hurts but what hurts is the broken expectation that you've held onto that says they should not be as they are. This again has nothing to do with the *other,* but everything to do with you clinging to the mind.

The mind can run with this and create problem after problem, saying, "Well what if this happens, or this, or that!" The point of this book is not to help you solve your problems, but is to help you see more clearly that the problems you *think* are there are not really there at all; they aren't even real!

The problem is a mental creation that stems from the fear that you might lose who it is you think you are. The invitation is to see that who you think you are isn't who you are, but rather a dream self that lives in the mind.

The problem that wants to be solved will never really be solved since it's wrapped around a self that isn't even there. So it appears that after one problem is solved, the mind will create a new one. Just as if you get an answer to your question, the answer will lead to another question; this is a cycle that has no end.

If you look at the honesty of others to support your wellness, you will find yourself mentally preoccupied trying to determine if another is being honest or not. Again, this is living in the mind and not in this moment.

Rather than being so concerned about what other people do or don't do, I invite you to use this energy to pay attention to the movement within yourself and taking place in this moment. If you do this, you will notice a guiding force that wants to lead you to your own wellness, which is independent of the actions of others.

> *The point of this book is not to help you solve your problems, but is to help you see more clearly that the problems you think are there are not really there at all; they aren't even real!*

Chapter 13
Health & Well-Being

I'd like to touch on the subject of Health and Well Being. It is a common assumption that your health is determined by what you do and don't do. I would suggest that your actions do not determine your experience of a healthy life, but rather it is how you perceive life that determines your experience of living a healthy life.

What you experience in the manifest world is only a result or an effect stemming from what happens within your perception. This is much the same as when sickness or dis-ease arises; the illness is actually a symptom of your *perception*. The more you focus on trying to change the symptoms, the further you ignore its actual cause, which is your perception.

In this case, you can see how dis-ease is an internal alarm that alerts you to your perception being off; it is a pointer that attempts to show you that you are out of alignment in how you dance with Life. Hear this clearly: do not be consumed with changing a *symptom*, but rather make the focus on changing *perception* which is the root of the experience.

If you were to go into a garden and pull weeds, the wise thing to do would be to pull out the entire root system.

For if you only pull off the tops of the weeds they will spring back in a matter of days. This is what happens in most people's lives as they attempt to bring healing, since what they try to change is just the symptom rather than going for the root.

If all we do is try to change the symptom, the root cause remains and the symptom will only transform into a different type of manifestation. You can see this everywhere in your life as 'problems' continue to arise even though you thought the problem was solved.

For example, if you find yourself to be overweight, you might be inclined to change this manifestation with an intense willpower. Since you only focus on the surface condition, you believe the condition is being caused by something on the surface, and you look outwardly to see what might be causing this experience of being overweight. Often, the overweight condition is contributed to the food you put in your body, which at this point in time is a common belief.

Something is being missed though as you are not seeing that perception comes *before* action. If you are set on a conquest to change the action and not the perception, you will find yourself in a situation where you are met with major resistance. This resistance often takes the form of trying to force yourself to eat certain foods or to exercise, while you feel empty of joy during the process.

The delusion here is massive; if you find that you can force the symptom into submission and change the surface experience without changing the cause, you will see that the symptom will re-emerge either as regaining the weight, or experiencing the dis-ease in a different form. The wise thing to do would be to uproot the cause, which is your perception, and allow the change to happen naturally and joyfully.

If your perception changes, re-aligning with what is True, the physical experience will reshape itself to match your desire or reshape itself to be in alignment with a whole and healthy life experience.

It's vitally important to point out that these experiences of dis-ease are only pointers that desire to show you the errors in your perception. This is much the same way as seeing relationship drama or pain as an alarm that goes off to tell you something is out of alignment. And like pointing fingers at your relationship partner, if you point fingers and blame your symptoms, you entirely miss the focus of the lesson.

Blaming the symptom is like blaming your relationship partner for your dis-ease, when in truth the relationship partner is free to be as they are. Just as the experience of being overweight is free to be as it is, and in no way it is wrong or invalid. Trying to change the symptom is like trying to change a relationship partner with the hope that this will create wellness or fulfillment again.

> *What you experience in the manifest world is only a result or an effect stemming from what happens within your perception.*

What is your relationship with your dis-ease? Do you despise it? Do you resent it? Do you fear it? Do you want desperately for it to be something other than what it is? All of this is simply a form of resisting Life and all its forms, not realizing that the form is only a result of your perception. Putting blame on the condition or resisting the condition, only blinds you to its cause, which quite sincerely diminishes your ability to correct the perception.

So, of course, the first order of business is laying down this fight that wants to resist what is being expressed. This can also be stated as Self-Acceptance.

Here you get closer to the root issue, the only reason such dis-ease would arise is because Life is trying to show you something important, something primary to your unfolding. In the example of being overweight, the vast majority of human beings want to be skinny because they feel that in being so they will somehow be more acceptable or worthy. They feel that if they were skinny or healthy, they would be more likeable, which in turn would somehow help them to like themselves. So this quest per se isn't about losing weight as much as it is about becoming more acceptable and therefore, more whole.

This is the mental delusion that creates the dis-ease to begin with. You have placed your wholeness once again outside yourself and given chase to something external to make you well. Because you do so, you become disconnected from Life through perception and your experience takes on the form of dis-ease.

You can see here that by trying to change the external, you only reinforce the condition or the dis-ease by proclaiming that if this external symptom were eliminated, you would be whole.

If you do find yourself forcing life into a box to change the symptom, the victory will be short lived. If the cause has not been dealt with, the dis-ease will have to resurface. It will have to take form again in some way or another because the reason for its appearance was to teach you something about your inherent wholeness. If the lesson was not learned, by Life's very nature another teacher must arise.

This cycle of dis-ease resurfacing time and time again is a testament to how important the lessons are to begin with. Over time, or lifetimes, the dis-ease can become more intense just as an alarm clock can seem to become more loud and abrupt over time. Sooner or later, these lessons will be learned and your imbalances, through a new perception, will become stabilized; it must, as it is the natural order of Life to do so.

The degree in which you experience the liberation that comes with these lessons totally depends on your willingness to see what is True without running from your imaginary fears. If you wish to hold on to your illusions about life, your mental dream, your insecurities, that is fine. However, sooner or later, holding on to the dream will simply become too unbearable.

You see this often as you crumble in tears or have emotional breakdowns, which are a result of the heaviness that comes with holding onto the dream. The energy builds up in such a way that eventually you fall to your knees and admit that you sincerely do not know. The challenge, of course, is questioning whether or not you are seeing the gift which wants to present itself, or will you simply construct another dream to hold onto?

For example, if you have a relationship that painfully collapses, do you look within yourself to learn its lessons, or do you run to another relationship where you construct a new story that temporarily brings a false sense of fulfillment?

If you were to correct the error in your perception, relationship drama would be an impossibility, regardless of whom you spent your time with. If you were to correct the error in your perception, internal dis-ease would be an impossibility as well.

I want to point out that healing doesn't always happen in the way you think it might, thus it is important to let go of the outcome of how you think healing should unfold. Genuine healing that is desired is actually a desire to heal perception, and not a desire to change conditions. What is meant by this is that healing is an *internal* happening; it is a movement where internally you feel whole, fulfilled, joyful and fully loved.

You are misleading yourself if you believe that this experience of wholeness will only come if the external conditions are changed. Therefore, you wait for a new manifestation before you allow yourself to be well. Meditate on this, if you will. Is the healing that you really desire an external condition, or is it an internal experience? If you desire to be skinny, is it really being skinny that you desire, or is it the internal experience that you believe will accompany a skinny body, such as a greater self-acceptance?

What would it matter if you were skinny, yet still felt unloved, unwhole, or unaccepted by all of mankind? This requires a heavy dose of sincerity. Most people would not want to admit that what they really desire is the internal experience of Love, as it might put into jeopardy the outcome of being skinny. To not admit such a thing is to reinforce the delusion that says your wholeness rests in the fulfillment of desire.

The only thing that is ever *truly* deeply desired in Life is the union with the True Self. Since you look at the manifest world to complete this union, you get lost in the world of form and this union becomes the most elusive of things. You instinctively know the union is there somewhere, however you are simply looking in all the wrong places.

As you recognize more clearly that your state of dis-ease is a result of perception and not the condition, you stop looking to change the condition, and start looking inward to find the root, the cause. If you look inward for the cause, it will be discovered with greater ease because you are now looking in the space where it resides rather than looking externally for the root where the root cannot be.

It's like looking for the weed's root on the surface of the garden. How insane! Imagine yourself frantically searching around for the root without getting your hands dirty and digging deep. Looking inward, looking at your perception is what turns the light on and when light enters the room it becomes much easier to see what is happening. When you see clearly the cause or the root, quite effortlessly the light turns on as the switch has been flipped and the internal experience of dis-ease vanishes or subsides.

It vanishes because its purpose has been served, which was to show you your mistaken perception and allow for you to see Life more clearly, seeing Self more clearly. Again, this is the point of all dis-ease: to show you something about how your perception of life, others, and the Self is out of alignment. So let us embrace dis-ease; let us embrace the symptoms, knowing that they don't define who you are, but rather are here to help you to realign.

Most human beings are afraid of these symptoms because they emphatically feel that the symptom defines who they are. People are afraid of being overweight because they believe it's a form of social rejection, which leads to personal rejection. In Truth though, the experience of rejection has nothing to do with other people but rather is a delusion you lay upon yourself by believing your value or worth is determined by the thoughts of other people. Silly humans.

If you carry this delusion in any form, it is Life's role to correct this error in perception by serving up that which you are afraid of, so that it may be seen and transcended. Or it can also be stated that it is your higher Self that serves up these lessons so you can enter into a more Realized Truth about your nature, about your True Self.

Isn't this what you want most, to be reunited with a Love you feel has been forgotten or lost? To be with wellness? To be accepted and whole? This is the primary desire of all human beings; it is programmed into your being. As you wake up, more and more this desire becomes deeply pronounced, and the pain of not uniting with it becomes more unbearable.

In knowing this deeply, you will embrace all that comes your way, be it dis-ease or whatever else chooses to arise in your experience.

To embrace this dis-ease doesn't mean that you have to like it; it simply means that you give it equal validity, or an equal right to be. Just as in embracing other people for who they are doesn't mean that you have to enjoy their company, but that you do grant them the same value and worth you desire for yourself.

Embracing only becomes difficult when you are trying to cast blame or judgment onto that which you are attempting to embrace. As you see clearly the innocence of all form, blame is impossible, and embracing is seen as your natural state.

Stand naked in front of the mirror and watch your mind go crazy; watch how it lashes out with judgments and condemnation about how your body is unacceptable, about how your body is less than perfect or lacking in some area. I'm not saying this just to say it; I'm inviting you to really do it.

Many people simply avoid looking at themselves all together and whether it is naked or fully clothed does not matter. It is the avoidance of looking honestly into your judgments, which is the issue, and it is a clear sign that you have become prisoner to the mind.

Far too long you have been bullied by the content in your mind as you see yourself as a tiny creature that is terrified by your mental dreams. The only reason this mental content can imprison you is because you fear it. So it is not the mental chaos that creates the bars of your prison cell, but is your own fear that keeps you bound.

The key to your prison cell is the Self-inquiry, the meditation, and the quiet investigation... that humbly stands before the fear with a willingness to see beyond its illusionary nature. Just as we've discussed already, it is the willingness to see the fear as a stick that looks like a snake.

This is much like watching a scary movie, yes you can become frightened, but deep down you know it's not real; you know there really isn't anything to be sincerely afraid of. At this point in time, I am personally not a fan of watching scary movies; it's just something that does not interest me. However, a while ago there was a movement within me to go see the latest scary movie playing in the local theater. I didn't really know why this desire was there, but I wasn't in any position to resist the desire so I simply followed the flow.

I made a point to watch the movie with a willingness to pay attention to my internal response to what I was seeing. What I noticed is that the more I bought into the story, the more I identified with it, the more afraid I became. The moments when I simply sat as an observer, the whole thing became a laughable matter.

You can see this take place as you stare at your naked body in the mirror. The more you identify with the thought that passes through the mind, the more you buy into the story being told and the more afraid and unwell you become. To simply be present as one who *watches* the thoughts without looking to have those thoughts identify you, what is noticed is an absence or decreased presence of fear. Quite often, these judgmental thoughts become laughable as you see clearly just how insane and untrue they really are.

This isn't to say that you should judge your judgments or push them away, but simply look to see if they are really true, or are they just a mental dream that stems from a lifetime of conditioning? Remember.... these thoughts that arise are just as valid as any other thoughts, none of which are actually true. What makes the whole thing problematic is that you buy into the story and look at the story to define you in some way; which is an impossibility.

> *Embracing only becomes difficult when you are trying to cast blame or judgment onto that which you are attempting to embrace.*

As you engage this practice of aligning your perception with Truth, the physical world or your manifested condition will change on its own. With the example of being overweight, as you learn to accept yourself as you are, releasing the fight that wants to blame and judge the condition, you find that your behavior changes automatically.

If your path to weight loss includes a changed diet and exercise, which it may or may not, what you will discover is that within you there is a shifted desire that actually *wants* to eat differently and be more active. Therefore, you will thoroughly enjoy the process of transformation rather than it being a journey that's met with resistance and disappointment.

This path of taking on a diet and starving your being from what it really wants *could be* an indication that you are still living with fear. In this you find yourself with tremendous guilt anytime a desire arises that wants something you have labeled as unacceptable. This movement only reinforces the root cause of non-acceptance, or looking for acceptance where acceptance cannot be.

Remember, what brings about this condition of being overweight is not the food you eat or don't eat; it is brought about by what is being perceived. Just as stress might be something that brings about dis-ease, it is not the *event* which creates the stress, but it is the story *about* the event. Again, it is your perception that creates the internal dis-ease which manifests in all sorts of surface conditions such as heart attacks, weight problems, cancers, and the like.

As a society we are hell-bent on healing symptoms as if they were the culprits, with no regard for healing the actual cause. This is only sprung from ignorance and it too has its place, so let us not find ourselves judging society for not seeing the cause clearly.

This isn't to say that you should ignore symptoms and let them go unattended. The point here is not to mistake the symptom as the *cause*, but to see the symptom as a manifestation of *perception*. You can see the surface condition as a pointer to something deeper, but yet may still find yourself moved to treat a symptom with conventional means.

The difference maker is your perception during the treatment of a symptom. If you treat a symptom while seeing it as a threat, or seeing it as not deserving of Love, you reinforce the delusion that brought the symptom about in the first place. Therefore, even if the symptom dissipates, the root cause is still present and Life must provide you with another symptom until the lesson is learned.

Often times, the lesson can be as simple as merely accepting the symptom as being equally valid or seeing clearly that the symptom is not something to be feared, but in Truth has every right to be present just as you yourself are here.

The things you fear the most are often the things that come into your life experience. If you fear poverty, then lack and scarcity enter your experience. Please see this clearly, you can have a million dollars in the bank and still have the life experience of lack and scarcity. If you fear sickness, you will experience it in some form or another. If you fear rejection, Life organizes itself to allow for this fear to make itself known. Not as a punishment, but so you can be Free.

> *To simply be present as one who watches the thoughts without looking to have those thoughts identify you, what is noticed is an absence or decreased presence of fear.*

You cannot sidestep fear with the hope of being without fear. You must walk through the fire of fear to know that the fire cannot burn you. To simply hear or read these words of wisdom means nothing if you are not willing to let the insight be the wind in your sail and move you up and out of the self-made prison of fear.

To merely hear these words, without a willingness to engage Life, will do nothing. You must put into practice the wisdom you know as it is the Movement of Truth that allows well-being to be experienced. So let Truth move through your perception.

Maybe now you are beginning to see the beauty in all things. Even the most violent symptoms are really a manifestation that wants to show you more Love. Just as when you view other people who might be violent, perhaps you can now see their violence as a call for Love. People only act out in ways that cause harm because of a perception that sees the self as limited, unaccepted, and unloved.

As you encounter these elements of life that arise, yet seem to be unpleasant, might we see their presence as a call for Love, as a cry for acceptance? In doing so, you will notice that such experiencing won't need to manifest in your life because you have accepted them as whole. Just as when you experience conflict with another person, the moment you accept them wholly and wish upon them nothing but absolute freedom, the intense drive within them to conquer you subsides.

A person's desire to conquer you is only sprung from a perceived inadequacy within himself or herself. So when Love is returned, it helps to fill the void; it sheds light where light was not. Can you be this instrument of Love, this candle in the night, this melody that sings of genuine freedom to all?

I understand that such a perception might seem foreign, or completely irrational. This is fine if it doesn't make sense; I'm not encouraging you to swallow it just because it is stated in this book. If anything at all, I'm inviting you to investigate a deeper element of Life, and the element in question is this Love I speak of.

> *You cannot sidestep fear with the hope of being without fear. You must walk through the fire of fear to know that the fire cannot burn you.*

Chapter 14
Money

If you haven't noticed by now, the remedy for all of Life's ills is quite simply a correction of perception, which has nothing to do with trying to change the external. As your perception aligns with the Truth of Life, all areas of your Life come into alignment with the abundant and joyful nature of reality.

In knowing this, addressing the subject of money will hopefully prove to be a short chapter. At first I hesitated writing on this subject at all, since most people are so caught up with the notion that more money will solve their problems. However, I think this topic can illustrate some points that will help us to live with a greater experience of abundance while doing away with the many misconceptions people have.

When I first started to write this book, I intended not to have chapter names for the sole purpose of encouraging people not to skip around looking for specific advice to certain 'problems', particularly about money. The book is laid out in such a way to take you through a process of realigning your perception. If one were to go straight to the middle of the book, it's likely you would miss some primary points that help to clarify the whole message. However, we chose to include chapter names for the sake of clarity, but I'm happy to be able to address the point anyway.

If you find yourself doing such a thing, skipping around in search of answers, which I have done many times with books I've read in the past. I simply encourage you to slow down. For a baby who is determined to walk before learning to crawl will only be met with frustration and disappointment. If he finds that he can walk without crawling first, he will miss an important developmental process that will take away from a pleasant walking experience.

To be so consumed with not crawling first is a clear indication that you feel your well-being is in walking. On the subject of money, focusing solely on its accumulation would be a clear indication that you believe your wellness will come in the form of getting more money. This misconception will only set yourself up for suffering as you again place your worth in some external experience.

Money, as with everything else, means nothing until you give it meaning. Even after you give it meaning, all you've done is created a story about it, and in no way does the meaning you give it actually define it; all it does is help you determine how your relationship with it will unfold.

From here on out, let us forget this *label* of money and focus more on the experience of *abundance*, since the word abundance is more inclusive and a better representation of your desire. Even with this word 'abundance,' there are many stories, ideas, and concepts about what this word means.

True abundance has nothing to do with what you do or don't do, it is rather your natural state as a human being; it is what you already are.

Abundance in the sense that I use the word might be described as, but is not limited to the experience of having your needs met with plenty left over to assist in the expression of your being. Abundance is not the experience of having a large bank account. For even the one with a large bank account can still and often times do experience lack, or scarcity.

The experience of lack and scarcity can be described as the feeling of not having enough, which is the predominant experience of most human beings. We have flipped this quest of abundance upside down by believing that if our external world were full of stuff or resources, internally we would feel content, safe, and whole.

> *True abundance has nothing to do with what you do or don't do, it is rather your natural state as a human being; it is what you already are.*

The more you try to heal the scarcity on a surface level, the further you reinforce the delusion that keeps you trapped by the bars of discontent.

The experience of lack or discontentment is a symptom, which points to your perception being off, or not in alignment with Truth. As your perception realigns and you see clearly your inherent abundant nature, life can't help but create a life experience that matches your perception.

Here you might find your mind going crazy as it asks questions like, "What about those who have lots of money but still see themselves as separate beings?" Or, "What about those who live in third world countries and have zero resources or opportunities?"

Such questions are irrelevant if such questions don't point to your own life experience. I say this because the insight in this book can only address *your* experience and not that of another person. Just as the insight another person might receive from this book has nothing to do with your life experience. What I can say, though, is these principles of perception are not biased or dependent on life circumstance. Just as gravity isn't biased according to gender, color, or background.

Each life experience that presents itself in your world is designed for your soul's growth, which unbeknownst to you was also designed by you, or more appropriately stated, designed by your Higher Self. So for those who find themselves in a life situation that they may despise, such as third world poverty, are actually going through a growth process that is vital for their soul to reunite with their depth.

Everything has its place. Whether you understand it or agree with it is irrelevant. Just as if you wonder why the leaves fall during the autumn season, whether you fully understand the leaves' role is irrelevant for life to continue on in the way that it does. I encourage you not to be so caught up with your judgments about the unfolding of other people, and rather focus more on correcting your own perception.

If you would like to gain insight into why you experience lack or scarcity, all that is necessary to see clearly is to notice your own judgments and perceived separation. When you judge something, you tell a story about it, and that story gets sent out via your perception, and life brings back to you a life experience that reflects your story or your perception.

For example, if you find yourself living in a small house that doesn't quite match up to your preference, notice how you judge those who live in a bigger house than you, or judge your own space as something to be ungrateful for.

If you find that your bank account seems to lack funds, notice how you judge those who seem to have more than you; one such judgment might be that rich people are better than poor people.

If you find that your current vehicle isn't to your liking, notice how you judge those who drive a different car than you, this might be a judgment such as.... people who drive nicer cars are more acceptable, or people who drive crappy cars or less worthy.

> *The more you try to heal the lack or scarcity on a surface level, the further you reinforce the delusion that keeps you trapped by the bars of discontent.*

The only reason lack and scarcity arise in your experience is to show you where your perception is off. If your experience seems to be one of scarcity, by default you are attached to a judgment that is pulling this experience to you with great force. The solution is not to rearrange the surface condition and work tirelessly with the hope of forcing life into your box, but rather the solution is to correct your perception and to allow Life to unfold naturally.

If you say that you don't have such judgments, but yet your experience reflects scarcity, I would say you're simply not being honest or are not willing to look deeply within yourself. Let us draw these judgments to the surface so you might see them more clearly.

These judgments I speak of are not just judgments that point towards other people, I'm referring to judgments, period; to believe something to be other than what it is. For example, and this is a good one so pay close attention, if you find yourself at a store and you see a price tag on something that seems to be more than you can afford, what is your internal response?

Do you look at this item and proclaim that it is *too* much and that the price should be lower than what it is? Do you judge the establishment assuming they are making too much? Do you get discouraged because you feel the absence of this product in your life means you are less than whole? What arises within you?

When you extend ten dollars for something, what is your internal response? Is it one of scarcity? With each piece of currency you extend, there is a story being told within your being, and it is this story that will determine your experience. This isn't to say that you should find new stories to tell per se but is an invitation to question the stories that you *are* telling and to determine if you are believing something that isn't true or something that reinforces a limited world.

Is it true that a desired product costs too much, or is this only your judgment? It's not the judgment itself that creates the limitation, but it is the belief in the judgment followed by the feeling that sends out the energy and brings back the experience.

Let's not forget that most people are out to add on to their identity through the acquisition of 'things.' The 'wanting of stuff,' with the hope that you will become more of something, more valuable or whole, is the driving force behind most desired purchases. So it might be wise to handle the issue of this identity before you get caught up in this quest for abundance.

As we've discussed already, this quest to become more of something is a path that leads to suffering because what you truly are is that which can become no more or no less. You are *already* whole and your suffering comes from the perception that something is lacking from what you truly are. As you look to a purchase to define yourself or to create an identity, you proclaim that in this moment you are insufficient in some way, and therefore you experience internal deficiency, or internal scarcity.

Is it true that getting what you want will make you more lovable, acceptable, or whole? If you can see clearly that it does not, as you have experienced many times in the past, then the anxiety you feel in not having what you *think* you want will diminish or dissolve completely. This again points to my hesitation in addressing the topic of abundance.

If you have not woken up to your True identity first, then this quest of seeking abundance can serve as a distraction to your Awakening. Please hear me clearly on this; when you wake up to your most Divine Nature, abundance/contentment is something that will flow naturally, without you feeling as if it is something that must be forced or acquired.

As you find yourself out in the world, when you find yourself 'wanting,' sincerely ask yourself, "Do I want this because I believe it will somehow make me more of something, or less of something?"

Spend time in this place of inquiry. Reflect on past desires that you *thought* would make you more whole but only failed miserably.

If you find that such a desire is rooted in the ego's quest to be something other than what you are now, see if you can lay down the 'wanting' without effort. If you cannot, then proceed in any way you feel led and simply, but honestly, pay attention to how the experience unfolds.

Such a thing isn't difficult to notice within yourself, especially if you are willing to see what is true.

Have you not had the experience where you see an awesome car, or house, and the first thought you have is about what other people would think about you if you had such a thing? To make purchases from this space, from the ego's desire to be noticed by others is only to proclaim that something about you in this moment is lacking, thus you create internal scarcity, which bleeds external scarcity into your physical world.

If you perceive that you are lacking anything in this moment, Life will offer up experiences that reflect your perception. So to move on behalf on this insecurity is only to reinforce the delusions, which create limitation in your world.

If genuine freedom is to unfold in your world, you must be willing to see your inherent freedom in this moment. If abundance is to unfold in your world naturally, you must be willing to see with gratitude your inherent abundance in this moment. This points to the power behind your feeling of gratitude.

Gratitude is an age-old principle that packs a powerful and universal punch. Gratitude represents a feeling of completeness, of wholeness and of wellness. Therefore, when you are with this feeling of gratitude, you project or perceive that all is well. In this perception, life gives back what you perceive. There is a real power here, a very real power that rests below the surface of your physical experience.

By contrast, you can look at the feeling of being ungrateful, of feeling as if there is nothing to be thankful for. What does this feeling project into the world, and what does this feeling do to your internal experience as a human being? Surely, it doesn't make for a pleasant existence.

The confusion here is that many humans believe that the feeling of gratitude, and the feeling of being ungrateful is something that is determined by external factors. Just as when you believe stress is a result of external conditions, you believe that the experience of gratitude is only going to happen if the exterior world can change as well. Again, this points to the backwards way in which you may live your life.

When you wake up to your most Divine Nature, abundance/contentment is something that will flow naturally, without you feeling as if it is something that must be forced or acquired.

I encourage you to let go of the notion completely that changing the external world will somehow improve your internal state of being. As you do let go, or allow yourself to see the Truth of the matter, you will undoubtedly notice a gentle calm that enters your being. You will notice many things, the most important of which is Liberation from wanting; since your wanting is primarily made up of wanting to change your exterior Life condition with the hope that it will end your suffering.

As you see with greater clarity that your experience of lack and scarcity is a result of your perception, and not a result of external factors, your entire world changes instantly. You no longer find it necessary to blame or judge as it pertains to other people or things; you no longer find yourself to be a prisoner of the external world, since you now see clearly that it is *you* who creates either a prison or a paradise and not anything or anyone 'out there.'

This is where the real work begins. I say the 'real work' since your old efforts of trying to change the external world through manipulation, judgments and will power are seen as tired ideas that lead nowhere as it pertains to uniting with the True Self. This 'real work' is the only work or movement that will affect meaningful change and the work is a work of perception, not action.

If you can discover gratitude for your current life condition, you have the necessary tool to rise above it. In a state of gratitude, you remain open to the lessons that want to move you into alignment with your inherent abundant nature. In a state of unthankfulness, you remain closed off to the lesson, as you believe your current life condition is without value and serves no purpose.

I'm not speaking about generating a feeling of gratitude for the abundance you *desire,* or focusing on what you want in the *future* and be thankful that it is on its way. The invitation is to sincerely discover gratitude for how life is *now*, in this moment. Can you see clearly how it is that your experience of scarcity is an innocent expression that sincerely wants you to reunite with your True Self, just as relationship drama is there only to serve your Awakening?

If you can see such things clearly, the feeling of gratitude is something that happens naturally. This Awakening process isn't about manipulating your being into feeling a certain way with the hope it will change your experience. That is simply another form of the mind's egoistic control that believes the self to be small and limited, hoping that a changed experience will equal a changed self.

As you see Reality clearly, truly beyond your judgments, such a thing as gratitude is something that arises without effort, without you having to do anything. The same goes for abundance which is the natural state of Life; as you perceive Life in accordance to what is True, abundance and contentment become your experience by default.

How else could a universe continue on in an infinite way if it was not abundant in nature? Resources are not limited but only appear to be limited since the collective perception of human beings is one of limitation, scarcity, and fear.

Have you not had the experience where doors just seem to open, leading to fulfilled desires? Or the experience of synchronicity that seems to support your movement? What I'm talking about is when Life organizes itself to support your every movement. This cannot happen if you see yourself as separate from life, which is what happens when you judge, condemn, blame, or find yourself wrapped in fear.

If you find yourself with a feeling of discontentment or unthankfulness, question it. Don't be so quick to identify with it but step aside and sincerely question whether or not this thought or feeling is stemming from something that is True, or is it merely a temper tantrum of the ego which is an imagined self that feels separate from all of life.

To get back to the point of the subject of abundance, let's go back to the example of extending money. If you extend money to someone or a business, and find within yourself a feeling of fear, scarcity, or emptiness, know that such a feeling will only bring about more of those experiences, which solidify those feelings. What you may find helpful is to simply wait until you can make the purchase from a place of gratitude or until the purchase just feels right... feels natural. Making purchases or conducting business from this space of wellness, or wholeness will create seemingly miraculous unfolding for your life experience.

Upon entering an establishment to make a purchase, discover a gratitude for the presence of the store as you enter. Discover a gratitude for the people who are working there so that you might have the opportunity to buy something that is needed or desired. Notice all the options you have in the store, and discover gratitude for them. Give yourself permission to smile at people, knowing they are free just as you are.

If you notice that what is desired costs more than what you currently have in your wallet or bank account, there is no need to be fearful; simply recognize that the funds are not yet available, and if you can't make the purchase right now, it obviously isn't the right time. If it bothers you that you cannot make the purchase now, it is a clear sign that you are with fear and believe the purchase will somehow make you more whole.

Do you see how Life is constantly trying to teach you? You can see this experience as an alarm that says, "Hey silly, you're trying to identify with this purchase. You are trying to find love where love cannot be."

Another question to ask is whether or not you see money as a limited resource. As you extend money, do you believe that in doing so your resources become less? If this is your belief, life will confirm it by creating more experiences to prove your belief as correct.

I encourage you to see money and resources as just another form of Love... which it is. With this perception you can convert money to something like Smiles. When you make purchases, see it as exchanging Smiles for other Smiles or other forms of Love. With this perception, you do away with the scarcity mentality that holds back money with the hope of hanging on to it.

How silly it would be if we were to go to a store and think, "This store wants one-hundred smiles for this item, but I only think it is deserving of fifty smiles." To think someone's price is undeserving or in some way wrong, is only going to reinforce the perception of scarcity. If you end up paying the hundred smiles, you do so with a fear that smiles are limited.

This was addressed in a similar way in the chapter about Love. Love is not something that is limited, but most people think that to have love they must withhold it from other people, or be careful about who they extend it to. To do such a thing only withholds Love from the Self, since Love is experienced only when shared. To withhold Smiles, or money from a place of scarcity is only to withhold it from yourself.

If you anxiously argue with someone over price with the hope of getting a better deal, you only withhold abundance from yourself. The trap here is that often you feel good when you convince someone to lower his or her price. This is only the ego feeling good about its ability to conquer another person or situation. It's a form of the ego adding to itself, but really what is being added is just an idea... an idea that says, "I'm more valuable because I got what I wanted." Really what happened, though, is that you withheld Love from yourself, you withheld Smiles thinking that it gave you more Smiles.

This isn't to say that you should not take advantage of discounted items. If an establishment offers up items at a discounted price, this is wonderful, as it can be perceived as a gift to you. The point in question is whether or not you are projecting limitation as you try to withhold money in the hope that it will give you more.

I thought about touching on the subject of being a business owner, but it seems that the above wisdom can be universally applied. Focus on your perception, and by you perceiving and embodying the Truth of what you are, the guidance needed will flow into your world naturally.

Nobody knows what you should or should not do; this is something that will come from within you. If you rely on others to tell you such things, then you might find yourself going down a path that isn't so much in line with what Life is trying to arrange for you. Many find themselves running from one seminar to another or one book to another, looking for something external to guide their lives.

Granted such a thing might create change in your world, however, the deeper change, the change that will matter most is only going to come from within your being.

> *The point in question is whether or not you are projecting limitation as you try to withhold money in the hope that it will give you more?*

Chapter 15
Following the Heart

The Heart's Song

What can be said about following the Heart?
... as I sit quietly I'm tempted to say nothing.
For when I speak to your soul,
the mind only hears words,
Just waiting for the chance to interrupt me.

So many thoughts you have,
Beliefs, opinions, silly expectations.
Sitting in your mind like an empty brick;
all weight, but with no real substance.

When might you be done,
Finished with this mental game?
Asking questions without listening,
Seeking thoughts of a different color,
Trying to avoid the end of your egoic flame.

The eternity you long for,
will never be found in the jungle of your mind.
Such a tool was not meant to discover the infinite,
So get off the mental wheel
of searching for what it cannot find.

This expedition is for the Heart.
A journey of a thousand Souls.
To reach that which is everywhere,
One must stop looking for Gold.

To hear the whispers of Life,
One must move with a new way of listening.
To hear the Heart and to follow its movement,
One only has to be willing, to give up everything.

We have all felt that tiny inkling which warmly turns in our humble hearts. Not the grandiose plans that scream from the ego with the sole hope of being better than the rest, but the gentle nudge, which desires only to express itself. It's as if a small voice says, "Yes, go out into the world and be yourself."

Mmmmm, what comforting words... Yes! Go out into the world and be yourself.

Be that movement that moves you. Dance as the wave but know you are the ocean. Express your deepest Self with colors never seen. Love with a reckless spirit and insightful eyes; give all that you are to all of Life so Life can give to you all that you are.

The only thing that makes following the Heart difficult is the fear that somehow you might lose who it is you *think* you are. As you get clear about your True nature, about what you Truly are, following the heart becomes a natural movement. It is not something you will have to *try* and do; therefore, I invite you to not make following the Heart some monumental task that must be conquered. Keep focus on the most important thing, which is waking up to what is True.

As the Heart turns and attempts to guide, you may get caught up in this game of worrying about an outcome. This, of course, is why following the Heart requires you to return to the unknown. The Heart's movement is not concerned with outcome; the Heart's movement is only concerned with being what you are in each moment. It is the egocentric mind that wants to solidify a particular outcome with the hope that it can secure its dream about itself.

Notice this movement within as you feel led by the Heart; watch the mind get caught up in worrying about an outcome or about how the outcome might put into jeopardy the false image of self. If within you is a willingness to die to this false self, by following the Hearts' movement you will discover the expansion of your True Self.

If you are concerned with the concept of failure, you have mistaken failure to be something that is unworthy, mostly because you have been conditioned to believe that failure diminishes your self-worth, and you are desperate to protect this imaginary worth at all costs. What is not seen though is that even if failure arises, this *too* is part of the journey for us to return home. Failure is the same as success, for each failure teaches or helps us to realign with that which draws us closer to what we are really after.

> *Love with a reckless spirit and insightful eyes, give all that you are to all of Life so Life can give to you all that you are.*

Remember, what is being sought after is a union with the True Self, not an inflated *idea* about the self which is what the ego wants, but a genuine return to all that you are. Failure is a requirement, and therefore, you are encouraged early on to accept the fact that failure is a possibility, and in failure there lies as much value as success.

If you negate failure and believe it to be less worthy, you simply resist the lessons that your Heart wants to lead you to. So embrace failure, let go of the control that wants only to validate success, for your effort to do such a thing is really just a ploy of the ego to sustain the false self. This, of course, is a judgment that says success is better than failure. Is that True?

"So many thoughts you have,
Beliefs, opinions, silly expectations.

Sitting in your mind like an empty brick;
all weight, but with no real substance."

As the Heart moves, your conditioned mind jumps into play with its beliefs, opinions, and silly expectations. All this mental movement is just a dream, but yet you give it validity as if its comments are actually true. You see your beliefs about failure being true, so you avoid Life's call. You see your opinions as truths, and ignore the Truth of this moment. You allow your expectations to create a tiny box, which limits the flow of Life. You do all of this with the sole purpose of protecting a self that is not even there.

"The eternity you long for,
will never be found in the jungle of your mind.
Such a tool was not meant to discover the infinite,
So get off the mental wheel
of searching for what it cannot find."

If you look to the minds' content to discover your True Self, it is like running on a hamster wheel while going nowhere, and quite sincerely you wear yourself out. Surely you've had this experience, of trying so hard to fulfill a desire that you become burdened and overwhelmed by the jungle of your minds' expectations. On the surface it may look like you are being worn down by the external experience, but really it is the strong belief in the mental chaos that drains you of your energy.

The one who is inspired by the Heart will find this movement comes very naturally, almost as if it is not 'you' who really moves, but something that moves on your behalf. On the surface, onlookers might see you as working tirelessly or exerting great effort, but in Truth there is something deeper that moves you.

"This expedition is for the Heart.
A journey of a thousand Souls.
To reach that which is everywhere,
One must stop looking for Gold."

To align with the True Self, one must give up the quest of finding something that is not here already.

Your efforts to find gold, or to find something that is beyond this moment is just another movement of the ego that believes the self can become something more if the right ingredient is found. Just as in your quest to control outcome is a quest to find something that lives in an imaginary tomorrow.

> *The Heart's movement is not concerned with outcome; the Heart's movement is only concerned with being what you are in each moment.*

The challenge here is that if you are so locked into your outcome, you limit Life's movement. Is it not possible that life might have something in plan that you are not aware of? Yes, letting go of the outcome might seem difficult as it induces fear. It might seem to be easier to create a fanciful story in the mind about how your desired outcome will solve your problems and all will be well.

If this is done, if you create such a story and cling to it, you are projecting that your wellness is dependent upon an outcome of tomorrow, rather than already present here right now. This, of course, leads to you walking a path where the journey can seem stressful, as you have gambled your well-being on some event in the future which you instinctively know you have no control over.

> *To align with the True Self, one must give up the quest of finding something that is not here already.*

Following the Heart isn't about creating well-being for tomorrow, but it is actually about allowing you the opportunity to do what the soul longs for. If you do not, you find yourself resisting this Heart movement, which only creates blockages as you live Life. So with great sincerity, I say that following the Heart is your natural movement, however, you are so preoccupied with the minds' dream you never fully engage in this moment.

"To hear the whispers of Life,
One must move with a new way of listening.
To hear the Heart and to follow its movement...
One only has to be willing, to give up everything."

To hear this call of the Heart, one must give up relying on something which is not true... the dream. This comes by way of questioning the dream, by questioning the thoughts, which attempt to keep you from moving in the direction you feel led to move. As you question this, you will discover that these thoughts do not comment on Reality, on what is True, for these thoughts only wish to serve an imaginary world.

To give up everything is to return to the unknown. You give up clinging to your mind's perceived outcomes because you know with humility that no one knows how Life should unfold tomorrow. Therefore you remain in this space of Truth. You give up the judgments that you cling to because you know that judgments can never be True. You simply rest in this moment knowing that the only Truth... is this moment, and the Heart moves *only* in this moment, therefore, you move in Truth. You let truth move through you.

This isn't to say desired outcomes have no place. Far from it. Desired or inspired outcomes can help to guide you. The difficulty comes when you cling to outcomes as if they hold some monumental importance to who you are, to your identity. By believing you will become more of something when the outcome is solidified, you see the self as separate from wellness. To let go of outcome doesn't mean that the desired outcome is not there; what is meant by this letting go is a recognition to the Truth that outcome is not going to fulfill you. So let us not look to outcome as if it is something that must be fulfilled, but rather it is a playful movement in the heart or mind that may or may not manifest.

> *To give up everything is to return to the unknown.*

If you are not looking for an outcome to add to the self, letting go of outcome is quite natural. Life teaches you if you are clinging or not. If you find that you are bothered anytime the perceived outcome gets threatened, it is a clear sign that you are looking for something that is not here. This, of course, is how Life guides you; if you heed the call that tries to show you that you are clinging, you drop the clinging and life can flood you with more insight into what movement you are to follow next.

However, if you do not heed the call of the internal alarm, the journey will simply be met with more resistance and suffering until you do. For most human beings, the alarm is never validated because you are so obsessed with getting what you want with the hope of being something more than you are now. The alarm is seen as a threat to your identity so you resist it, not realizing that the alarm is innocently trying to be your guide.

It's been a common practice of mine to ask myself two questions anytime I am met with the need to make a decision. These questions are as follows:

1. What are my options?
2. In what direction does my Heart move?

Followed by the willingness to... Let go of outcome.

What are my options? In any given moment, you are presented with forks in the road: paths that you can choose from. Yes, it is true that you may never know which path is the right one or the wrong one as it pertains to reaching an outcome, but again this isn't the point to know something that cannot be known. The question remains; what are my options?

The questions are not, which option is the right one, or wrong one? The question is simply what are my options? Be clear here, I am not asking what paths might I take or want to take, for these are speculations and hopeful expectations. Surely we can all come up with actions that we might want to take, but whether we really take them or not is altogether a different matter. You might find yourself making a list of hopeful actions that deep down you know you would never do; most of the time these lists are about actions you can take in the future and not actions that can be taken in this moment, from your Heart.

As you ask what your options are, ask on behalf of this moment and on behalf of your most sincere Self. Life wouldn't ask of you anything that you are unable to do, or anything that is not possible in this moment. As you layout your options for this moment, which might take thirty seconds or an hour, sincerely ask the question, "In what direction does my Heart move?"

Initially you might be bombarded with insecurities, judgments and the like, but remember to hear the voice clearly; you must clearly see this mental noise not as Reality but as a dream of conditioning. As you face these fears, you begin to see through them and their grip fades as mere background noise.

If you find yourself unable to embrace an option and move forward, then this simply is a sign that you are not ready for such a movement and you can choose a different option that feels much more natural.

Oftentimes, there is the fear that says, "What if I start down this path but can't finish it?" This again is the ego's attempt to control outcome, or solidify a false self, not realizing that maybe there is the possibility that you were never meant to finish it, but only to extract wisdom from the experience while you were engaged in it for a short time.

If you walk in this space of the unknown, you will find that the right insight comes at the right time; the appropriate doors open at their appropriate time. Likewise, certain doors might close as well. This doesn't mean that you failed, it could simply mean that the learning on this path has come to an end and it is now time to move in another direction. It is very possible that Life might move you down one road with no intention to complete it, but only to gather wisdom that will be used in another direction.

There is tremendous wisdom here. As I've stated already, there have been many times in your life where you thought you wanted something so badly, only to find out that you were glad it never worked out; perhaps a particular career path, a new business venture, a relationship or the like. Have trust in the unknown, trust that all things are working together for greater good. When you trust this, you will discover a detachment as it pertains to outcome;

resting as joyful now in this moment rather than looking to the next moment to fulfill you.

> *Life wouldn't ask of you anything that you are unable to do or anything that is not possible in this moment.*

As you engage these two questions, the most important part is the follow up statement, 'the willingness to let go of outcome.' This simple willingness will have the most profound impact on your ability to flow with life and to reach greater depths of being.

What might be helpful to illustrate this point are personal examples. Let's look at my experience of writing poetry. Growing up in the public school system, I did relatively poorly compared to most other students. I actually found myself dropping out of school and not finishing, which was due to my inability to follow an outline that other people provided for me. One of the areas I was proficient in failing at was writing and literature, which could also be said about most other subjects, except art classes and physical education, which l loved. I had zero interest in being able to do something I simply wasn't interested in.

As I grew older I felt within me this inner nudge to write, I didn't know what to write, but I felt the nudge nonetheless. When I was about 26 or so, I started to write short articles that pretty much just expressed my own internal growth from an egocentric standpoint. It was me, or ego, trying to make sense of what was happening within me. What I noticed quite quickly is that I *could* write; in the sense that I was able to construct complete sentences with relatively correct punctuation and deliver a point with ease.

I was a little shocked, a little dumbfounded. I didn't question the ability much because I was simply enjoying the process. A short time after I started writing, I found myself writing poetry. This I found to be a little bothersome considering it put into jeopardy my false self-image as a masculine human being.

This insecurity didn't last long because the joy of writing poetry was much more fulfilling than trying to uphold a self-image that didn't feel natural anyway. Writing poetry on the other hand felt incredibly natural and effortless.

I ended up sharing these poems on a website I created which garnered little web traffic or eyeballs, yet such a thing didn't bother me much because I wasn't writing with the hope that others might take notice; I was writing because I enjoyed the process.

I remember several occasions when I would abruptly wake up in the middle of the night and experience extreme anxiety over the idea that I put poetry on the Internet for everyone to see. I thought, "Holy shit, people are going to think I'm some kind of pansy. What kind of person writes love poems about Life and then shares it on the Internet where it may never go away?" This, of course, was the ego's last-ditch attempt to protect a self-image that was fading into the background.

Can you see how these thoughts are delusional in nature, how they are attempting to protect some future idea of self? Their only purpose was to support a dream, not to support Reality or my True Self.

This truth was blooming within me as I embraced this new expression that wanted to explode within, the insight came to show what was true; that being... what I am is something beyond what other people think of me, beyond what I think about myself, beyond thought itself, and what was most important was that I heeded the call of my heart.

Even as I write this book in the moment at hand, I don't write because I want something in return, I write because writing is what wants to happen in this moment. I fully acknowledge that this expression may never leave my office space, may never be read by anyone other than me, which is fine because I'm not looking for approval from others to validate my worth. I don't need other people to validate my expression, since I already know it's valid, simply by the fact that the desire is here and now.

If life chooses to do something with this book, and you find yourself reading it, great, but it has nothing to do with my little idea of self. Likewise the value you find in this book has nothing to do with me for I am not the one who interprets from your awareness. In addition to this, if you find that this book smells of sulfur and disgust, this too is your perception and has nothing to do with me. I am merely a melody being played by life, I am the Life that moves in this moment and my only call is to hear the melody.

Therefore, I don't find myself being stressed out over the progress of this book, when it should be finished or should not be finished. It simply doesn't matter because I have no attachment to its outcome and in this I find a free flowing love that seems to write these words without effort.

I've had experiences where I felt anxiety about *needing* to write a book instead of *allowing* it to flow from my Being, and when I imagined the end result I got overwhelmed. "Where the hell do I begin?" I would anxiously question. "Do I create an outline of the whole thing...? Oh God, how the hell do I do that?" Such anxieties didn't last long because I would question if the thoughts of anxiety were based on Reality or on some dream to protect a false self.

Now as the movement moves, I find the book writing itself, in a way that I would have never imagined. There is no guilt trip for not writing on certain days when I had hoped I would. There is no solid expectation that says it should happen this way or that way.

A couple of years ago I had the pull in my heart to write my first book, which ended up being a collection of wisdom filled poems, one liners, and the like. When the first desire came about, I knew that a book wanted to be written but I didn't know when, how, or where. I didn't know what kind of book, how big or how small; I just knew there was a movement to write something in a book form.

A year had past and I thought... "What the hell, no book." Then a short time later, it hit me like a two year old who unexpectedly smacks you across the face. What I didn't realize is that the book had already been written and was just waiting to be assembled.

You see, that whole time I was *waiting* to write a book, I was following the flow and writing poems and short wisdom quotes that filled up my journal. There were about 600 wisdom quotes and about 30 poems that I had written with little to no intention on turning it into a book. From there I went through all these quotes and poems and picked out what were thought to be good ones for a book, a process which only took a few days and seemed to flow like nothing I've ever done before.

In addition to this, the process of getting the book printed and self-published was incredibly joyful, and the resources to get this done just seemed as if they dropped into my lap. I was able to get hundreds of books printed without going into debt, and share these books with a small group of people who were waiting for me to write one.

To this day, the book hasn't done anything that would be counted as extraordinary by the masses, but again it doesn't matter because that's not why I wrote it. I've had tons more fun giving away more than I've sold. I see it as a gift from Life that I'm able to share with others.

> *I am merely a melody being played by life, I am the Life that moves in this moment and my only call is to hear the melody.*

This perception that isn't caught up in the game of making sure I sell them all to make money, contributes greatly to the abundance I've experienced in other areas of my business life. I'm not locked into the idea that just because I give books away that it should come back to me in the form of being able to sell more books.

I simply allow Life to give back in the way that it sees fit, the fruit of which has gone above and beyond anything that my egocentric self could have ever orchestrated on its own.

What has been learned or realized deeply is that Life sincerely wants to take care of us, to fulfill our Hearts' calling, to nurture our expansion and to help us all along the way. Because of this, I find it easy to let Life do what it does, and I simply do what each moment calls for, which is whatever the Heart feels moved to do.

Life isn't concerned with your ego's desire to be noticed or validated. This is simply for the reason that Life knows your egocentric self to only be a dream. Life might move through the ego, as the ego can be seen as a tool to function in life, but Life isn't on a quest to help you build the worth of that which is only a tool. That would be like you wanting to help your toaster to feel good about itself... to feel like it is better than all the other toasters in the neighborhood, hoping it might make better toast. How silly.

> *Life isn't concerned with your ego's desire to be noticed or validated.*

This same approach that pertains to my writing is the same approach that is used when engaged in things like running a business. At this point in time, and it could change at any moment, I run a business from my home office. This business is the form of expression that Life created for me to move through with the purpose of supporting myself and those that I care for.

If you ask other people who work in the industry that I do, whether the way my business was built is a good model for others to follow, they would laugh hysterically. If you were to show them the fruit of this venture I am engaged in, they would simply count it as being lucky.

Even I myself might count it as being lucky if I was not aware of the underlying movement of Life that has allowed for such an experience to unfold. If you believe that luck is something that falls on people in an unorganized fashion, you leave your own desires up to chance while you believe yourself to be disadvantaged in some way if your desires never manifest.

What I have been most amazed with, time and time again as I continue to live Life, is that my best movements are the movements that are born of the Heart. I say this because when you move on behalf of the Heart, you are doing what it is you really want to do. When you do what you really want to do, you live life with less resistance. If you find yourself constantly engaged in something that you deeply do not want to be doing then you are simply gripped by fear and live with tremendous resistance.

As has been expressed many times, living in a state of resistance blocks the flow of Life that wants to guide you, and this is the internal state of most human beings. We all experience this in some degree or another; the point is that as you loosen the grip on fear, or live with less resistance, it is like turning the faucet little by little to allow a greater flow into your being. If you find that your faucet seems to trickle out water, turning it up would mean that you face your fears and see through them.

Since fear is the dominant expression of humankind at this point in time, it may seem as if there is a secret ploy to keep you bound in fear by other people. There is some relevance to this, but let's not get caught up in the actions of others. Discover your own Liberation, in the way that it simply doesn't matter if someone else tries to keep you locked in fears' frequency, for this can only be done if you accept the fear as outside yourself, as some would want you to believe.

To empty or heal the internal fear within you, means that no one can manipulate you through fear.

In my experience of following the Heart, I notice how backwards my movement must seem to the onlooking ego.

This, of course, points to the backwards way the ego wants to live, for of course it must be backwards, as the ego believes it can find itself in an inside-out manner. Meaning, it looks for self in the external world and moves as if it can find itself in some other place than now, or some other place than in reality.

Don't plan on other people accepting your Hearts' movement. Their judgment about how you live your life is only a judgment that reflects their dissatisfaction with living their own life. So if anything, their judgments are only a call for love as they desperately want to accept themselves and their own decisions.

If you find that you encounter such judgments from other people and it bothers you, then let it point to the delusion of believing that the thoughts of other people can define what you are. These judgments will bother you if you are looking for other people to validate who you are. If you look for others to accept your movement as a human being, you are surely setting yourself up for resistance and suffering.

This is what is meant when we talk about standing on your own authority. Look within your own heart for validation, rather than in the mind or thoughts of other people. Rely on the Truth of you, of this moment, of what is real rather than the mental dream that pervades the mind of humankind.

There is no need for this new way of listening to Life to create anxiety. Anxiety is only created when you feel as if you are not doing something that you should be doing, along with believing that who you are will not be fulfilled unless you do something other than what you do now. This is to miss the point. Following the Heart is about doing what you can in whatever way presents itself in the moment. If you find yourself not doing something, it is clearly not Life's plan for you to do it, in this moment.

Yes, you may find that it will be done in some other moment, but let us allow each moment to take care of itself. There is no room on this journey for condemnation. There is no legitimate reason to judge your non-action. To judge it is to believe that your wholeness is determined by what you do or not do.

> *When you do what you really want to do, you live life with less resistance. If you find yourself constantly engaged in something that you deeply do not want to be doing then you are simply gripped by fear and live with tremendous resistance.*

I'm not suggesting that you simply lay down all your responsibilities and give up automatically all the ways in which you live your life now; that is to take this message to an extreme and negate the human element of this whole process. The point of this wisdom about following your Heart is to let in what comes naturally, and simply be willing for the insight to move through you and do what you can with what you have in this moment.

> *Following the Heart is about doing what you can in whatever way presents itself in the moment.*

Chapter 16
Perception Dancing

Living Life and allowing this Love to explode from within you can be characterized by the illustration below.

Above is an expression of Life, which at first glance appears to be a tired old lady who looks like she just drank a cup of spoiled prune juice. By turning the image upside down, by changing your perspective, you notice something different entirely. What was once thought to be a bitter old grandmother has transformed into a beautiful princess.

What changed... the expression, the external, or your perception? Is it true to say that this is an image of a sad old lady? Is it true to say that this is an image of a beautiful princess? In Truth, they are neither. One could say that the lady is not sad, but only tired. One could say that it is not a beautiful princess, but a stuck up bitch with a crown.

What is vitally important to notice is that what you look for you will see. If you look to find something beautiful, you will discover beauty and whether she is young or old does not matter. If you look to find disgust, you will find it in the old and the young as well. The expression, however, remains how it is, regardless of your opinion about it.

The power here is that your experience with the image, your relationship with it is determined by how you choose to see, or by what it is you look for. It has nothing to do with the image itself, for the image is just an image. So as with Life... every experience is just an experience, neither good nor bad, neither pretty nor ugly. If you look for beauty in a particular moment, Life will bring beauty into your world. If you look for scarcity, life will bring it into your world; or rather you will create it in your world.

Beauty truly does rest in all things, whether it is a personal failure, an unkind grocery clerk, a mid-life crisis, or all the times your dog pees on the carpet. Just because we cannot see it, doesn't mean it's not there. Just as in the example illustration, it might be possible that you couldn't make out the image of a princess, yet just because you can't make it out doesn't mean it's not there. The moment you do find beauty in the most unsuspecting of places, you'll shout with joy and say, "Oh my, how could I have ever missed this?"

It's much like holding a coin in your hand and realizing that there is something to be perceived on both sides; the most important of the realization lies within the insight that *both* sides are completely valid. Here is where you may get yourself into trouble. You see, you have fooled yourself into the false belief that only one side of the coin has worth, therefore, you reject the side that you deem as invaluable.

Imagine you had an expensive coin with both a princess and a witch on either side, you look at the princess and then turn the coin over, to your disgust you see a witch, because you might not like witches you throw away the valuable coin.

This simple act of rejecting that which you do not prefer, or labeling it as having no value is a form of resistance, which only energizes the side you deem as unworthy. Now, every time more coins come into your experience you look to make sure it is witchless, not realizing your disgust is irrelevant to the value it holds. Your judgment robs you of your worth.

If one side is rejected, life must restore balance by bringing the rejected aspect of life into play until it is accepted as completely valid.

On the collective level we push against poverty as if it has no value, and because it is rejected, it becomes intensified in our experience. Pushing against violence as if it is something that should not be is not realizing that violence is only a symptom. The true cause of violence stems from the perception that you are separate from life, and therefore, must protect your separate self, or protect your dream.

You can see this more clearly by using an example of a scab on your body. Even though the scab might be unsightly, or undesirable, it serves a great purpose in healing. If you were to pick at the scab, or resist it, it then by nature becomes more pronounced, more problematic. The focus here is not to get rid of the scab, but to understand more clearly how it came about.

If you see that the scab is a result of you not paying attention while engaged with Life, you learn to be more aware while letting the scab do what it needs to do... which is to facilitate healing.

At first glance, you might not be able to see the beauty of the scab, but again just like the illusionary image, the beauty is there if you remain open to see it, rather than being so fixated on getting rid of the image or expression as if it had no value.

You would think that as a collective race, we would learn that a movement such as war really does not solve anything; we use war as a disguise to push against that which we have been conditioned to be against or to resist. However, the more we push against it, the more we separate ourselves from it, and therefore, we experience even more war.

> *If one side is rejected, life must restore balance by bringing the rejected aspect of life into play until it is accepted as completely valid.*

This is simply a testament to our asleep way of living, and the suffering will become more pronounced, the war will become bigger with each passing moment we choose to not see the true cause, which is our perception of self as limited and separate from Life. The solution of which, and hear this clearly is not that we desire for other people to wake up, or for other people to see clearly, this would only be a form of not giving freedom to other beings to learn their lessons in their own time. The real solution, the *only* solution is for you to wake up to the war that rages within yourself.

A similar example is in trying to change a relationship partner, in which this fruitless attempt goes nowhere.

Trying to force or impose a lesson on someone else is really just another form of judgment, of resistance, which puts you in a position where you restrict the flow that wants to liberate your own soul. The collective war is only a manifestation of the war that exists within the individual.

As you become aware of the war that takes place on a collective level, let this be a sign to see the war within yourself. If you find that you proclaim that there is no war within yourself, yet you believe the war of others is wrong, or should not be, you simply have not yet healed the war within yourself. More importantly, as you empty within yourself any war, or resistance, you will find it to be impossible to engage in other peoples' war, herein lays the solution.

The external wars in your world that seem to bring about so much suffering can only go on if people buy into the judgment that is being shoved down their throats. Even if you burned up all the weapons, but if within your heart is this judgment, this condemnation that proclaims some people are better than others or more/less deserving of love, war would once again rise up. So here you can see clearly that trying to change the external condition through laws, wars, and condemnation really changes nothing if the heart of the One who perceives does not change.

This is one reason why activism can seem to be something that either goes nowhere, or only creates temporary change. The traditional form of activism is to oppose one side of the coin while proclaiming your preferred side as the best one; this only energizes the side you are against as you focus energy on trying to get rid of it. This type of activism is only a reflection of the division or separation within the heart of the activist. It is an expression of the non-acceptance towards life.

If you are to engage in activism, the wise approach is not to stand up for what you are against, but it is to hold your attention on that which you are for, while fully accepting the other side of the coin, acknowledging that it too has its place. If you have difficulty in understanding how this might be, all you must do is look at all the commotion in our world that is focused on *changing* conditions rather than first *accepting* them.

You exert tremendous amounts of energy and resources trying to change conditions that only seem to become more pronounced with each passing moment. Whether it be disease and sickness, war and famine, relationship drama or the like. The more you try to change external conditions without first healing the false perception in your own world, the condition only seems to get worse.

> *The collective war is only a manifestation of the war that exists within the individual.*

How is this possible, to be *for* something and not *against* something else? It is simply a matter of clearly realizing that the undesirable side is not bad or unworthy, but is simply an expression that is trying to teach you, rather than seeing it with judgmental eyes that want only to condemn it. If you entered a store and the only two available items for purchase were either peace or war, you could simply choose peace while leaving war on the shelf.

You understand that another soul might choose war because they have not yet learned to be without war. This expression of war is where they feel led. Because life is trying to teach them to be without it. Just like while trying to learn how to ride a bike, one must be willing to experience pain, even though the pain is undesirable. Sooner or later you learn to ride without falling down, but if you negate falling down and judge it as something that is wrong, you simply stay off the bike and never learn to ride it.

To live with peace, you must being willing to walk through the fire or war that rages within yourself. There are no shortcuts. So as you see others fall off the bike of life by experiencing suffering through such things as war, rather than condemning their actions, see it with compassion; just as you would when watching a loved one fall off a bike. How silly it would be to say to them they are wrong for falling off their bike, or that falling off is something they should not do.

If you condemn a loved one for their inability to ride a bicycle like you can, does this help them to learn and grow? Or does it only reinforce an inadequacy, which creates resistance and limits the flow of insight that wants to help them move through the fire, and expand? As you hurl out insults towards politicians and fear mongers, you only reinforce the perceived separation that is the real cause. These insults only add to the war, by creating a new war that doesn't want to accept their life expression.

The help you provide others doesn't just come in the form of the actions you take, for if you move to help others while at the same time condemning them, the action goes nowhere. The real help is going to come by way of perception. If you drop two quarters in a cup of a homeless man while perceiving him as deficient or inadequate in some way, you only reinforce homelessness.

If you pick up trash while condemning the one who litters, you only reinforce litter and by default will experience more of it. If you attempt to correct a child while holding in your heart an unwillingness to accept their actions as a valid learning experience, you only reinforce the action that brought about suffering.

Living in such a way can be quite frustrating as you move around with so much action but yet nothing ever really seems to change in a meaningful way. You become tired, worn out, and discouraged as you are convinced that the solution to your suffering is in changing some external condition; which again is to proclaim that suffering is caused by the external world, rather than something that arises *within* you.

I commonly hear people say, "Geeez, I so wish I had known this years ago." What is not seen is that if you had read this insight ten years ago, you simply would not have been able to incorporate it into your experience. Just as some will begin reading this book and lay it down counting it as complete non-sense. If you find this insight to be valuable in the moment at hand, it is simply the right time, which gives you plenty of reasons to be grateful for your past experiences as they have all led up to this moment.

> *To live with peace, you must being willing to walk through the fire or war that rages within yourself.*

The point of living life in an Awakened state is that you live with less separation, and by default you live with less suffering and more Love. As you do so, the change you desire is something that happens seemingly on its own. If the perception changes, the manifestation changes. If the perception is fear based, the experience becomes fear based. If we perceive love, then love becomes the experience.

It can seem like a magic trick of sorts, but so can the flipping of a light switch if you are unfamiliar with something as common as a light bulb. It's not that this is something mystical but it is that you simply are not familiar with the genuine movement of Life, the genuine movement of your True Self. As you become more familiar with true perception, everything that I am addressing in this book will become clearer.

True perception can be likened to an inner technology. If you got into a time machine and went back a thousand years, something as simple and common as a telephone could be seen as something that could only come from the heavens above. But in Truth, the potential for such a technology has always been there, yet what wasn't there a thousand years ago was the understanding of how to make one or how to use one.

What is even more interesting is that a thousand years ago this technology would have also been seen by some as something that came from the pit of hell, or as something to be condemned as it presented a new way of seeing Life. Such things are condemned because they threaten the old ways of seeing, and since there is attachment to these stories, the fear of change inevitably comes with it.

You can see though that having a telephone or internet can make for a richer life experience as you can stay in touch with loved ones from a distance, or share ideas at a much faster speed; we become more connected. This is the same movement as improving your perception to be more in alignment with Reality. There will be those who feel threatened by it and those who embrace it. This technology of true perception is a tool that leads away from suffering, and to a more realized state of being that creates a love filled existence.

In addition to this, the technology of seeing clearly is the most direct method for effecting change. Yes... you can try to effect change through might, willpower and condemnation as you create stress, suffering, and a shorter life span, or you can align with life and allow for change to happen on its own.

The choice is yours, you are free.

It can also be stated that this is the natural evolution of humankind, to be able to live with greater ease, beauty, and love. In the past, people of a different color would be hung as others gathered around to watch, cheer, and project their insecurities onto people who simply chose a different life expression. Now how absurd is such a thing? People wonder how such a thing could ever have been done. Today bombs are dropped on families in other countries with the hope of killing one person, and tomorrow we will collectively look back and see how compassionately absurd it was.

Likewise, tomorrow you will look at your relationship drama, your scarcity, your fears, and laugh compassionately as you see such a thing was only sprung from a mental confusion that wanted only to protect a pretend self. This is just like looking at your personal past and laughing off some of the choices you made as you realize that they were only a result of not seeing the bigger picture.

Undoubtedly, as you take on this quest to see clearly, you will be met by what seems to be resistance, or difficulty. You will notice that your whole world begins to change. The relationships you are engaged in might change, your current life path will seem to shake with uncertainty, and other people will definitely think you are crazy. Let such concerns be so light that they are carried away with the wind. Your fear of such change is only the effect of the effort in holding onto an illusion that wants to be protected.

Just as in worrying about what other people will think about you has nothing to do what you really are; the life conditions you want to hold onto, really don't serve your well-being as they are not the True Source of your internal joy. It's much like having a job and getting fired, initially we might be gripped by fear believing that our well being is now put into jeopardy, not realizing that life is simply trying to move you in a new direction.

If you allow yourself to be gripped by fear, the flow of this new direction will be cut off or restricted. When this new direction is realized, when the path is seen clearly, you will be cognizant of the truth that getting fired was a good and necessary thing as it pertains to your waking up to your most Divine and joyful Self. So why not just embrace the change from the beginning rather than being so desperate to hold on to your dream? Embracing this new movement within you will make for a much easier transition. Trust in the unknown; trust in the breath that gives Life to us all.

> *If the perception changes, the manifestation changes.*

I'm reminded of an experience I had years ago, where I was working for a company and temporarily got put on the night shift. I was scheduled to work from ten pm till six am, all by myself.

My duties included monitoring audio feeds that were playing over the radio and to ensure that the pre-recorded audio programs stayed on the air. Suffice to say, at first I was kind of excited about the idea, but after a couple nights, extreme boredom set in as it was a rare occurrence for anything to go wrong.

Rather than dealing with the situation in an honest and truthful way, I found myself taking off around eleven pm for a couple of hours and walking down to a friends' house who lived close by. I would hang out with friends while knowing in my heart that I wasn't being honest, and that in a way I was quite sincerely stealing from my employer.

No, my supervisors never caught me and no one ever knew what I was doing, but that doesn't change the fact that in my heart I knew that something was off. I was perceiving reality in such a way that proclaimed dishonesty as necessary; I was holding onto judgments that justified my unwillingness to be honest. I would say in my mind, "If I speak up and tell my boss that this night shift doesn't seem to be in alignment with my being, there is a chance I might be fired."

The delusion here is the belief that my job was my source of sustenance; I believed that my well-being was determined by the life expression rather than Life as a whole. Because of this, I did what I thought would protect my well-being, I chose dishonesty. What really wanted to be protected though was my false self, my dream world; in this dream, my worth and livelihood were determined by my job, which I *believed* that to keep my worth, I must do whatever I could do to keep my job.

This projection or way of perceiving saw the self as a little and separate being which must struggle and be dishonest to survive, and whose well-being hinged on the external. Because of this, my experience in this job turned out to be complete drudgery. I was dissatisfied and blamed the external condition rather than owning up to the truth that the dissatisfaction was a result of me not being honest with myself about the possibility that this job or night shift might not be a good fit anymore for my Soul. I was simply resisting life, resisting the movement within me and compensated my internal dis-ease by trying to manipulate the external world through being dishonest.

The most profound part of this whole experience was how Life brought balance to my dishonesty. Around the time I started to steal from my employer by ditching work while still on the clock, I noticed a stream of what could have been seen as bad luck. There were three incidences that I recall quite clearly, the first of which I locked myself out of my car and had to pay someone to come out and unlock it. The second, I locked myself out of my house and had to pay someone to come out and unlock my front door. The third, something randomly broke on my car and I had an unexpected expense to get it fixed.

At first glance, these things might just seem like common occurrences, but somewhere deep within me I knew otherwise. I took out a sheet of paper and wrote down these expenses and added it all up, I then made another list of the hours I stole over the course of a month and added it all up. "O ... M ... G (Oh My God)," I thought to myself. The total of hours stolen equaled the amount of money I had to spend on these unforeseen events.

I immediately stopped skipping work. I owned up to the realization that my experience of lack was a result of perception, however, I didn't use such language at the time as I wasn't as familiar with the workings of Life as I am today. I simply realized that I was creating my suffering; it wasn't life trying to screw me, it was me screwing myself by not being honest.

What I discovered, shortly after, is that by communicating my frustration about my current schedule with my boss, he was able to switch me back to a normal schedule as someone else was interested and waiting for my current time slot. Geeez.

Surely you can find such experiences in your own life in which you discovered dishonesty as something that didn't serve you like you thought it might, but rather only made living life more difficult. It is not because life wants to punish you, but rather it's because life must bring all things into balance. It may seem as if this makes for a vicious cycle, as dishonesty leads to suffering which leads to more dishonesty to avoid suffering. It's like telling a lie and having to tell the same lie day in and day out so that you might avoid the consequences that you are attempting to hide from.

This is spawned by the silly idea that the undesirable consequences will somehow threaten your well-being, which, of course, places your well being in external conditions once again. As I became aware of the consequences that I couldn't run from by paying for unforeseen expenses, I saw these consequences as fantastic teachers. It was Life showing me that by being dishonest with myself it only created suffering, regardless of anybody else knowing or not knowing about my dishonesty.

You can't run from Life, and you can't hide either. Each and every time Life will bring itself back into harmony; you can embrace such a thing and align with your most honest self, or continue to run and experience the snowball of suffering that expands as it follows you. If you embrace your inner honesty, which is to say that you embrace your True Self in the moment, suffering subsides and your experience is one where you flow with Life in a sea of well-being.

As you live Life, these lessons that lead toward Love are all around you and will be seen clearly if you are willing to see them or more appropriately stated, if you are willing to be honest with yourself. Your honesty might not lead to the end result or outcome you are hoping for, but it will always lead towards what you are truly searching for, which is union with the True Self.

It is similar to being a people-pleaser. You spend so much energy on trying to please others, or to ensure that others like you, that you completely ignore your inner call to do what you want to do rather than what other people want you to do. What you will discover quite quickly if you are practicing awareness and are willing to see the Truth is that trying to please people will never lead you to the experience of wholeness. The ego promises it will, by way of telling you that if others like you, you can like yourself, but time and time again your efforts are met with failure.

If you are living asleep, you simply *try* harder by doing what you can to please more people or to have more people like you. All the while this form of resistance to Reality blocks the flow that leads to where you really want to go, which is home... to your True Self. This, of course, is why suffering arises as you engage in such silly things as trying to please others with the hope they will approve of you. You are suffering because it is Life telling you that your perception is off the mark.

The suffering will become so intense, in this moment or the next, in this lifetime or the next that your soul will simply have no choice but to wake up and see clearly. If you reject the suffering and count it as invalid or wrong, you will simply have to repeat the lesson until the suffering is embraced and seen as completely valid.

> *I simply realized that I was creating my suffering; it wasn't life trying to screw me, it was me screwing myself by not being honest.*

This honesty I speak of doesn't mean that you go back and try to correct all the dishonesty in the past by pulling out your address book and trying to *right* a hundred wrongs. This honesty is about your internal state, which has nothing to do with other people. If you find that you are led by the Heart to engage another person as you heal, this is fine. But to condemn yourself by saying you will not experience healing unless you *do* something or take some physical action is a judgment that only reinforces delusion.

True honesty is about perceiving Truth, it is about correcting your perception rather than about doing the right thing. This is partly because there is no action that is right or wrong per se, since all action comes from perception. Also, there is no perception that is right or wrong as one form of perception is more valuable than another; there is only True perception or perception that is in error. If you heal your perception by aligning it with Truth, the right action will flow naturally without being blinded by the egos' false judgment.

True perception leads to an effortless action that supports Life and is wrapped in Love. False perception leads towards a resisted action that separates life and is wrapped in fear.

The choice is yours.

> *If you heal your perception by aligning it with Truth, the right action will flow naturally, without being blinded by the egos' false judgment.*

I'd like to put out a caution, or a yellow flag, and let it be known that as this insight enters your being and you find it to resonate with your soul; surely the ego will attempt to hijack the experience. One of the most dominating ways it does so is to turn this insight into a game of worth. It will say that since you seem to know something profound, it must mean that those who do not know it are somehow less than you are. This creates a sense of superiority in your being, as you feel exalted above other people.

Even if you don't believe this superiority complex is there, I invite you to keep a sharp eye out for it because it probably is there and you're just not seeing it. To have the perception that others who are without this insight are somehow less deserving, less valid or in some way dumb, is one way in which the ego supports its own imaginary self. One of the clear signs that this insight has become embodied is that you will notice that there is no longer the need to compare yourself to other people.

In addition to this, you see other people with the same worth and value as you have recognized within yourself, regardless of how their life might unfold. If you hold on to the delusion of the ego that you are now somehow better, I assure you that your progress will be stifled.

Another trap is that often times as this insight enters your being and you have an experience of total bliss, all your conflict drops and you enter a space that seems profoundly peaceful. Shortly after this, in almost all cases, this sensation of well-being will dissipate and it will seem as if you have been transported back to an asleep hell you thought was long forgotten.

This can be quite disheartening or discouraging as you thought that something was achieved and will forevermore be sustained as your new Life experience. This, of course, comes to the most common of questions by spiritual seekers. "How do I sustain this profound experience? How do I ensure that I always feel totally 'blissed out' and in complete awe of everything?"

The simple answer is that you can't. The one that wants to sustain such a thing is only an ego that wants to identify with an experience. You want to sustain total bliss because you want that blissful experience to become your identity. You don't want to be defined by your hell anymore, but want to be defined by some experience that seems so wonderful.

What is not being seen is that no experience can define you. You are that which comes before experience. By holding onto the belief that the self-made hell can define you, this is the perception that keeps you bound to it. If you are afraid to be without peace, you must go through non-peace until you are no longer afraid of the illusion that says the experience of non-peace can define you.

Can you see that by Life's very nature your effort to run from something only ties you to it all the more? This points to the very real Truth that you can do nothing as it pertains to waking up. If you run from suffering, you are tied to it. If you run towards bliss you are tied to that which you run away from.

The point is to **stop** running. Stop trying to get away from Life, from this moment.

Your most peaceful nature will emerge when you stop running, when you stop trying to be something other than what is showing up in this moment. You don't like this because you want to be in control, but hear this clearly; that which wants to be in control is an imaginary self that is afraid of losing its dream world. Every effort to gain control over Life is an effort that puts you back into a game of separation.

> *If you run from suffering, you are tied to it. If you run towards bliss than you are tied to that which you run away from.*

If you really knew your connection with Life, deeply, there would be zero desire to control anything. For how could that which is everything want to control something separate from itself. It is like a wave wanting to control the ocean, not realizing that it *is* the ocean. If the wave desires to *control* the ocean, it is a clear sign that it sees itself as separate from the ocean, and therefore, its life experience is lived as feeling separate and internally unfulfilled.

The wave mistakenly believes that if it reaches the shores of Fiji, it will somehow be more worthy. So in this, it tries with great effort to control the ocean with the hope that it touches the sands of Fiji. If for some reason the wave makes its way to its desired outcome, soon after it crashes on the beach, discontent sets in as the feeling of being void and unworthy remains and it finds itself being pulled back into the ocean.

What is not recognized is that its desire to feel whole or worthy is a direct result of not recognizing that it is not a separate wave, but it is with absolute Truth, the ocean itself. What might also be noted is that its desire to reach 'Fiji' is a desire to reach an idea and not an actual place that exists in Reality.

The wave creates an image in the mind that Fiji is somehow better than somewhere else. It tells a story about how reaching a certain destination will complete its being and totally validate its separate self. Is it true though? I'm reminded of ancient saying that points to such a Truth in this way... "The only peace you will find at the top of the mountain is the peace that you bring with you." Peace is an internal experience that has nothing to do with external conditions.

You can see this even more clearly with the following example. Imagine yourself being captivated by a sunset. Within you is this warmth that feels simply amazing and profound. Your mouth slightly open, but nowhere are the words to describe how you feel or what you see. Have you ever had such an experience? Have you ever experienced such beauty and peace where it seems as though time disappeared?

Where did all of this take place, this experience of peace and beauty? Did it happen in the sunset, which is outside you, or did it happen within what you are? If you contribute the peace and beauty to something that happens *in* the sunset, by default everyone that looked at the same sunset would have the same experience. Is it not true that there could be someone standing next to you as you gaze out into this splendor, but yet have a completely different experience from you?

Or what if you were consumed with judgments, fear, and resistance while viewing the sunset? Might it be that such an experience would not have happened at all and you would have counted the sunset to be just another boring setting of the sun?

For such beauty and peace to be experienced, it is up to the one perceiving and not up to the external condition. The beauty and peace that are seen while looking at the sunset have been there all along but what makes the difference is that you are willing to see the beauty rather than being preoccupied by the dream of judgments in your mind.

The power is not in the sunset, the power is in You. Remember such things as you find yourself running to find peace or running to find love, no sense in trying to find that which is already here. The invitation is that you see peace and beauty as already present rather than something that must be found in some other moment than now.

> *Every effort to gain control over Life is an effort that puts you back into a game of separation.*

If you find yourself falling out of this state of peace and well-being, or bliss, don't fight it, don't try and change it, embrace it as a necessary movement of Life. The funny part is if you find yourself attached to these blissful experiences by means of suffering when you are not experiencing them, it is a clear indication that there is more learning to be done. Therefore, you must enter back into the dream state to extract insight and wisdom.

Every unpleasant experience becomes more pronounced when you resist it; when resisted, you enter the realm of suffering. You can experience intense physical pain and still have an overwhelming sensation of peace during the process. However, this peace is diminished with each ounce of resistance you allow to be perceived.

Years back I blew out my left knee playing a game of tennis. It was the most intense pain I had ever experienced, even more than the time I fractured my spine while pretending to be a super star rollerblader. The pain quite sincerely felt like someone took a shotgun to my kneecap. Initially my ego took the biggest hit as the mind told stories of how my tennis days were over, and I could look forward to a life of non-movement.

Over the course of recovery without surgery, since I had no medical insurance, it seemed that my life was doomed as I was quite sincerely now playing the game of being a victim. Often times, I would find myself trying to get out and do something active, only to find myself on the ground screaming in pain as the dislocation of my knee seemed to be a requirement anytime I jumped, moved side to side, or turned directions without coddling my knee.

Over time I began letting go of the resistance to this external condition. I just accepted that this is how it is, and even though I might not understand why it happened, it happened, and there is nothing I can do to go back and change that. As this willingness to accept Life set in, I felt a renewed energy rise up within me. I still had to be cautious with my knee, but something was different.

The next time I re-injured my knee, the pain was there but this time the suffering was not. Without the suffering, without the arguments about what was happening, the pain wasn't nearly as intense. The moment I would fall, I would accept that pain may arise, and if it does then that too has its place. So I would sit with the pain without fighting it.

As life went on with this new acceptance, I embraced the unknown. I didn't know if I would ever do something active again. I let go of the idea that the only way I would be semi-functional was to pay for a surgery I simply couldn't afford. I let go of the silliness of the ego that wanted desperately to be defined by my ability to be athletic. I stopped looking for healing in tomorrow, and healed my perception in this moment by releasing my judgments that simply were not true.

A couple years after the incident as I grew into this new perception, I found myself doing things I never thought I would do. Granted, these new things came with experiences of pain and failure, but I offered up little resistance. I didn't believe that I should be able to do something that I simply wasn't able to do in the moment that presented itself.

I started to hike lightly, doing only what I felt comfortable doing, accepting any outcome that came my way. Long story short, since then I've been able to hike a ten-thousand foot mountain several times, something I thought was impossible even before my injury. My life now isn't defined by a knee injury, nor do I find myself being limited by any problems that still might arise in my knee. Even though today I can afford the surgery, it simply isn't something I feel led to do.

I learned a lot from that experience, lessons that have transferred to other areas of my life and made for a more enjoyable life experience. To say that I wish I could go back and not experience this injury simply sounds absurd. The suffering was never in the experience itself, but rather the suffering was in my non-acceptance of what happened.

> *Every unpleasant experience becomes more pronounced when you resist it; when resisted, you enter the realm of suffering.*

Chapter 17
Absent Conclusion

I don't know how to close out this book, to create an end where there is no end. From your space, your perspective, maybe there are many questions still left longing for answers, maybe there is contentment, or maybe sadness. And I would say all are appropriate.

Whatever has happened in our time together, in our moments of sharing, whether we be raised up with the freedom to let go, or burnt by a truth that shatters the false self, we remain as we have always been; completely whole.

The way that feels right, in this moment to close out this expression is to share a small collection of insight from my personal journal that I've written over the past year or so. This shall be my exit. But before I go, I'd like to say...

From the depth of my own humanness and not from the space of specialness that some might mistakenly believe in, Thank You and I Love You. In the most humble of ways, I am You, and this that I write is written for the Self that I Am. May we share in the Love that gives birth to us All.

Cheers to your most beautiful soul.

Insights...
by
T i g m o n k

Be As You Are

If I am with Sadness,
Does this mean I am not
the movement of the One?
Or does the One experience sadness,
Because the imagined Self
is becoming less,
The illusion... coming undone?

If anger slowly arises,
Does this mean
I am no longer the Divine?
Or is the Divine innocently having a dream,
mistakenly sleeping,
believing there is something
to protect and find?

There is nothing
that is not, everything.
No movement
deserving more or less Love.
For it is all Love,

Even the misunderstanding
...the forgetfulness that sees self
as a broken Dove.
And what makes life so unbearably fearful,
is the thought that somehow you must change.
Believing life won't accept you as you are,
Even in your masquerade of pain.

But Dear Child...Divine creature of light,
It is your own lack of self acceptance
that gives birth to your silly delusion.
It is you chasing an imaginary self
that blinds you to the Love
that rests beyond the illusion.

Be as You Are.
Allow life to be as it is.
For you are the Love in life that lives.
Dear One, be well
and remember this.

Tigmonk

Asking me how I connect with divine wisdom, how I receive profound insight from the universe is like me asking you..."how do you breathe?"

T i g m o n k

Give attention to this...

The desire for control is natural, however, the idea of self cannot control because it comes from a place of fantasy. So any control it thinks it has is illusionary in nature.

The real control you long for is the control the real You is always with, never separate from. This control is the force that moves the stars and rotates the Earth. This control is the movement of the One, the movement that balances all things. To be with this control, sincerely, is only found when the idea of self gives up all illusionary control and the real Self falls into the nature of Self, which is to embrace everything.

Through embracing all things, you will see with deep clarity that All is under a supreme control. Thus there is no need to control anything, for it is already done.

T i g m o n k

What keeps us from living the truth we know? The idea that somehow you're getting it wrong. You are the Truth. Regardless of how you live.

T i g m o n k

It is all happening on the inside of what you are. Your whole world, your entire human experience takes place within what you are.

There is no-thing on the outside, you are all of it.

...every argument.
every joy.
every frustration.
every smile.
...every judgment.
every compliment.
every fear.
every love.

There is nothing real that exists separately from what you are.

T i g m o n k

Being a Human Being is about *Being* a Human Being. It is not about being the human you think you should be; it is about being whatever arises in each moment.

Tigmonk

Truth is easy.

What's difficult is our resistance to the truth.

What makes Living Life so difficult is our constant quest to be in some other moment than this one. Feeling as though the 'self' is unworthy in some way... in a way that prevents you from just feeling Free.

The Truth Is you are Free.

The Fear that argues with your freedom is a fear that argues with nobody. The argument in your head that says you can't be yourself, you can't express the core of your beingness is an argument that falls on deaf ears . YOU are the One who is Here, experiencing this presence of humanness. This is your trip through. You... Create.

To be divided in mind about what you are, about what arises in your experience is to miss the point of this tool called the mind.

There is no little real-self to argue about in the mind, that self is just a story, there is only the Life that is happening in this moment. You Are Free.

Right Now.

In this Moment.

Feel it.

And then forget about it.

                    ... Because you will.

                    T i g m o n k

You don't know Tigmonk.
You only know an idea.
A very dangerous idea.

The danger is in believing your thoughts about who or what you think I am. Spend a day with me, and surely I will destroy many of your "holy" expectations. lol

I understand the confusion though, especially as I sit before you in Satsang or write about poetic beauties. These expressions do not point to the type of person I am in personal expression, they point to a stillness that lives in all of us. But nonetheless, I experience Life as a human being, and like you I express myself in ways that are sure to find judgment if watched with judgmental eyes.

As I sit with you as Tigmonk, I (intend to) sit with an absence of personal/separate identity (ego), an empty pallet of sorts, an empty space that makes room for the divine to share a message that I feel moving through this space that I am. If you watch me, you don't see the 'me' that functions in everyday life, you see an empty something that Loves wholly.

When I go back to my world of humanness, absent of intentional teaching/sharing... my presence, my way of living is surely different than any expectation you would create after seeing me share in Satsang.

So don't think of me as something 'better than' or 'more than,' it is only a trap that separates you from the Beauty I point to.

Why bring up such a thing? Because after sharing in Satsang, I see it in the eyes of the student, the look that wants to cling to an idea of Tigmonk. I am not that idea. Nor do I desire to have others see me in an elevated way, it is pure nonsense that goes nowhere.

This isn't to say it is wrong or should not happen. Sometimes such a thing can be natural and helpful. I simply share such a thing to bring clarity, and wash away any delusion that says you must be like Tigmonk to see the depth of your most Divine Self.

Tigmonk

As long as there are those who war with themselves internally, there will always be a war in the external.

The "world" (your perception of 7 billion people) was never meant to know peace in the future because peace has been present the whole time.

From the outside looking in, to see the forest from a distance you see a beauty that covers our land. A Peaceful image that captures our moment and humbly reminds us that... All is Well.

However... when you go deeper into the forest, to see the inner workings, you see all kinds of wonderful *and* frightful things.

You see animals killing animals and water soaked with the dead. What you witness here is a blooming; a Perfect unfolding that allows for an opportunity to expand and evolve as a conscious expression of Life.

True and Lasting Peace is not something for every person to experience at the same time. It is not a creation of something that is not already here. True and Lasting Peace is what Is already present, and the expansion or... the Blooming is the waking up to this Presences that sees the Whole Forest.

Your efforts and wanting for the exterior or for other people to change so that you might experience true and lasting peace is a great delusion that keeps the mind in a game of chasing a freedom that you have just given over to the exterior world.

In your own world, in this moment, in your present awareness of being, Peace is present. The only reason this peace would not be the present experience is because you are proclaiming that a better world exists in some other moment than this one right now. And the hoped for moment or world is one where other people do what you want them to do, so as not to jeopardize you dream of self... your comfortable ideas that you hide behind to help your ego feel safe.

Regardless of the life experience we may find ourselves in, it is always teaching us, or showing us the barriers we cling to that obstruct the vision of our Heart.

So whatever arises in this Life, in this moment, be it inconvenience or be it death, welcome its presence as a masterful teacher. If you condemn it, you turn away from the lesson it points to within yourself.

This, of course, is why we blame. We proclaim there exists no peace because of what "they" do wrong. Not really seeing, or being afraid to see, that our non peace is only a reflection of our internal war.

Tigmonk

Watch the scent that flows from your lips,
do you see how it smells of separation?
Always willing to reaffirm the divided,
to chase the mistaken.
Allow the end of this silly game.

Tigmonk

lol so much material "knowledge" on how to get what you want, but yet little wisdom into what this "you" is that wants what is not so desperately.

Tigmonk

The invitation is not to have better thoughts about yourself, the invitation is to see clearly that what you are cannot be touched by thought, period.

——T i g m o n k——

The absolute beauty I see in you,
is a beauty I also see in what I am.
Thus, I don't need your beauty
because what I see is also what I am.

Without needing what I see in you,
I see the fullness of you.
If I needed what I see in you,
it could only be because I see the beauty as limited.
Therefore I experience this limitation within myself.

T i g m o n k

What does it mean to rest in this moment? Well... Watch how much mental and emotional energy you invest in trying to get away from -this moment- and this will become clear.

What does it mean to let Life move you? Well... Watch how your motivation for living is sprung from an idea of self, from how you can build on who you are thought to be.

Is this not clear?

Tigmonk

You cannot have Trust... & Expectations.
It doesn't work that way.

Tigmonk

Just watch. Just watch the mind become obsessed with figuring out how it can protect the imaginary self through manipulating the external world. Shaping opinions, Judging the ugly, & Hiding in Silent Deceit.

Just Watch.

There is something about the real You that rests behind all of this noise. There is something about You, you need to know.

It is time to wake up.

Tigmonk

When you no longer seek getting ahead, or becoming more of something, life changes entirely. Behind this facade that constantly feels inadequate, there is a meadow that rest in complete wholeness.

Tigmonk

You don't run from life conditions, you run from your thoughts about life conditions. How silly...This is like running from nothing

Tigmonk

the door opens, say I.... "how may I serve?" the lost say.... "where am I going?"

When you truly arrive in now, you recognize that all there is, is service.

Service to an idea of self, or service to the reality before you.

To serve reality is to be present and to share that which is loving within you.

To serve an idea of self is to be tied up in the mind about tomorrow and yesterday, while scheming of ways to validate your story.

Tigmonk

What hurts most in life is not the events, but our unwillingness to accept what is. What hurts most is our resistance to the peace that is always present.

What's so funny is that you really think it's possible for other people to dislike you.

Tigmonk

When you see clearly that all your external relationships are a reflection of the relationship you have with your self, it will become evident that no one or no thing is responsible for how all your relationships unfold. In this, blaming becomes irrelevant, and what becomes more important is how these external relationships point to a deeper relationship between you and life or between you and you.

Tigmonk

A butterfly just punched me in the face. Or maybe it was trying to kiss me.

What is it that keeps you from following the heart?

Fear.

It's a fear that says I might lose who I think I am.

But dear one, the loss is only imaginary.

Try it and you'll see. This is the path to awakening to a deeper you, it comes by way of testing the cloud like limits. Which are not limits at all, it is just a mental confusion that has falsely imposed limitation on that which is infinite.

If we cannot see that all is well, it can only be because we are preoccupied with serving an imaginary idea of self.

You'll notice, if you look, all anxious thought or internal arguments only arise to protect an imaginary idea of self.

So why do we keep holding on to that which is only imaginary?

Why are you hell bent on protecting that which is not real?

Because, you're scared.

..and that is understandable, and acceptable.

But when you're ready, ready to lay it down and see what happens, Life will be waiting with open arms to show you that everything is going to be just fine; even without your dream.

Behind the anxiety, the fear of the unknown, rests only Love.

Promise.

Tigmonk

Do not walk ahead of the seasons; Life cannot renew itself if we are unwilling to let all the leaves fall.

Honor the unfolding of this moment by fully allowing the wind & rain. Do not give more importance to the sunshine, for if we do, we simply hide from the darkness within ourselves.

Tigmonk

Loving what is becomes quite natural, when you are not holding on to mental arguments.

Tigmonk

What confuses many, as it pertains to waking up to our most divine nature, is that most of us are waiting for some event or mystical experience to take place before we allow ourselves to completely let go; it's as if we are waiting for proof.

Waiting for proof is to proclaim that the goodness of you is not already here. This is why it is not experienced because it is projected in to some future moment. There is nothing mystical about enlightenment, about Love, or about what you are; it is very simple.

The simplicity is this... All your efforts to hide, hides nothing. Stop hiding and you will see that nothing is lost. When you condemn Self, you hide. Accept the Self, and you will see that condemnation was and is not necessary. In the absence of condemnation, Love will unfold within you.

When we are dishonest, we attempt to hide ourselves from the sun.

As we hide, we turn away from Love, believing that we have become unlovable.

Watch your hiding; watch how when you hide you condemn the self. Then ask, "is it true, what I'm believing about my Self, or am I creating suffering because I'm unwilling to accept myself in whatever form that might arise?"

Please allow me to clarify.

When truth speaks through me, it speaks from the vantage point of truth, not from the vantage point of personality. It is easy to confuse such a thing by believing the personality of me is the perfect embodiment of the truth I speak about, meaning that in some way my life is lived without resistance or challenges. This is not the case.

We all experience life lessons and challenges, relative to where we are on our individual path. To think that someday when enlightenment happens you will no longer experience difficultly in your unfolding is to delude yourself and keep the Self in a state of suffering.

This path of awakening isn't about being free of challenges; it is about seeing more clearly that these challenges are not a threat but an important lesson for our soul. In seeing this deeply, our life experience is lived with less resistance and more joy, but in no way does it mean we will avoid life challenges. We simply experience a freedom to allow life lessons to unfold more naturally.

Each person's life challenges are equal to the challenges of everyone else.

— T i g m o n k —

Living Life is effortless.

Arguing with Life, takes tremendous effort.

— T i g m o n k —

Does your wanting of something proclaim that you are without something?

In truth, there is nothing you are without. Wanting, creates the illusion of separation, which leads to a life experience of feeling unwhole.

Rest in wanting nothing, and discover the fullness of this moment.

T i g m o n k

The nature of truth is that you cannot be told what it is; you cannot hear its name. It is an unspeakable presence that Loves... everything.

...it is here right now.

Feel it as ever present.

now rest

T i g m o n k

The embodiment of truth is what matters. Your efforts to know truth only in the mind means nothing. Walk with caution as you go about being impressed with your seemingly important knowledge. Genuine freedom comes by way of living and breathing truth; it does not come by talking about what you think it is.

Tigmonk

If we are to embrace the true Self, there must be an embrace of Life as a whole. To embrace segments of life is to divide and reject parts of the self. To reject parts of the self is to cut off the self from the whole of life. Consequently, our life experience reflects separation rather than unified wholeness.

Tigmonk

Trust - is not something you give other people, but rather it is an acceptance for how life chooses to unfold.

Tigmonk

When you are done caring about what other people think of you, you realize how irrelevant your thoughts about others are; then hopefully, you might discover how pointless your thoughts about yourself are.

Here you may rest without judgment, and with a quieter mind.

T i g m o n k

The one who desires to see deeply into what they are, must first be willing to walk the path that shows them what they emphatically are not.

T i g m o n k

The fear of letting go lasts as long as it takes you to let go.

T i g m o n k

When thought comes knocking, I don't come rushing to the door because I know it's not for me.

T i g m o n k

Pay attention to those moments when you feel like withholding Love from life or others. Question what it is you are afraid of that leads towards you wanting to withhold Love. Notice how what you are afraid of is **losing** some element of who you think you are.

This fear that wants to withhold Love, points directly to your illusion of self, the false self that is separate from life. Notice how this false self is only imaginary. It only exists in your head, not in reality, not in now.

When people push your buttons, what they push on is your illusions.

Let it be a gift that helps you to awaken from your dream.

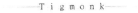

The only thing that is lost or gained in life is a dream.

Your experience of loss and gain is a story told in the mind, having nothing to do with reality.

There is only God, there is only the One.

This isn't to say that the One shouldn't experience this dream, it's simply to clarify that your identity cannot be touched by this dream; so there is no need to chase gain, or run from loss as if it can define you.

Tigmonk

Your life questions will never fully be answered.

Yes, there will be times when the answer you have will suffice, but the **unawake** mind continues on as it creates more questions. Do not hold onto the idea that if you had the answer, all **would** be well.

Letting go of such non-sense will keep the mind from forming so many useless questions that bring about anxiety and inner chaos.

T i g m o n k

This is it, this is the ultimate life... right now

Life will never be more than it is right now.
The fullness of what you are is here and now;
do you see it?

If not, it can only be because you look for it where it is not.

To see it, you must be willing to give up everything that is not in this moment.

The fullness of Love, a heartfelt completion of Life, exist**s** right now.

If you wait for it, you won't see it.

T i g m o n k

The Color of All Things Beautiful

If you are waiting for life to happen, you are like the fish who anxiously waits to find water.

Tigmonk

Would you like to know for certain, and without doubt, what you should be doing with your life? Would you like to know what your purpose should be, with great certainty? Well, here is the secret to such questions.

Look up, down, then all around. Wherever you find yourself in this moment is exactly where you should be. It is this moment that calls for your attention, your love, your being present and alive.

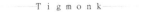

Tigmonk

I don't take sides because the line you think that divides is only an imaginary one. To take sides would be to believe the line is real, which only results in the creation of more perceived division.

For the one who truly desires the truth of reality, Life dares you to Remain the Center of it All.

The Truth is... I don't know how or why I do what I do.

Tigmonk

I simply just know that I am here. And in being here, there is a movement that moves me.

I quite sincerely just show up, and Life does what it does. The challenge I see is that we spend so much time resisting life, so much energy arguing with reality. If we would relax the kicking and screaming, and loosen our grip that tries to control everything, there would be a deep **seeing** that Life is trying to support you.

Tigmonk

The undivided mind is a mind that exists without argument. Wherein each moment the yes is yes, and no is no. There is no mental movement that argues with what is.

Most people are constantly unsure about their movement, wondering if they are doing the right or wrong thing, which only brings about suffering as one is never comfortable in this moment.

Give up the quest of doing the right or wrong thing and simply do what feels natural, and trust that your natural movement is your highest movement; which it is. Right and wrong are undefinable dreams based on one's conditioning, they will never be absolute. Therefore, their existence is not an actual reality but only dualistic movements in the mind.

———Tigmonk———

There is no finding the self, there is only the recognition of what the self is not. For you have always been what you are, and have only convinced yourself you are what you are not.

Rather than engaging a quest to find yourself, be open to discovering the untruths you have used to define yourself, others, and life. As these delusions fall away, you will see more clearly the beauty of what you are in this moment that's independent of judgments or comments from the mind.

One of the biggest challenges here is allowing ourselves to admit our insanity that wants to divide and judge people's worth based on comparisons, rather than seeing that we are all simply doing the best we can based on our own life experiences.

As we fall into this space of acceptance, we release the fight that believes life must change in order for us to be whole and happy. The feeling which creates our inner turmoil is this resistance I'm speaking of, the resistance to how life is unfolding in this moment

When we open ourselves to embrace Life's movement, Life can't help but rush in and support our awakening. For it is the natural movement of life to awaken unto itself, for you to awaken to your most divine nature.

Tigmonk

Problems are mental creations, not life actualities. If you believe in your problems, you empower them.

Try seeing them as situations that may or may not need your attention, without an attachment that says they can threaten your well-being.

Tigmonk

Freedom's Witness

If I want the butterfly
to land on me,
Then I proclaim
that it is not free.

For if I want
what is not,
Then how can I
Love and let it just be?

Openness is
The only solution.
For it extends Freedom
In all directions.

If it Dances,
I let it Dance.
If it Sits,
I let it Sit.

If it Rests
On my Being,
I let Life Rest,
No need to capture
What has been seen.

Why would I Cling,
To that
Which was Meant to be Free?
Why would I want
What is not,
As if I could
Somehow complete me.

Openness,
The remedy in Emptiness;
Extending to all of Life
I Am Freedom's Witness.

The End

Tigmonk

39114671R00168

Printed in Poland
by Amazon Fulfillment
Poland Sp. z o.o., Wrocław